NOV 28 2

PLYMOUTH PUBLIC LIBRARY
PLYMOUTH, MA 02360

DISCARDED 296.445
ABR

HEALING THE LOSS OF A PARENT
THROUGH JEWISH RITUAL

NECESSARY

MOURNING

DAHLIA ABRAHAM-KLEIN

PLYMOUTH PUBLIC LIBRARY
PLYMOUTH, MA 02360

Necessary Mourning
Healing the Loss of a Parent through Jewish Ritual
By Dahlia Abraham-Klein

© 2016 by Dahlia Abraham-Klein. All rights reserved.

No part of this book may be reproduced or utilized in any form or by any means, electronic or mechanical, including photocopying, recording, or by any information storage and retrieval system, without permission from the publisher or author.

Although every precaution has been taken to verify the accuracy of the information contained herein, the author and publisher assume no responsibility for any errors or omissions. No liability is assumed for damages that may result from the use of information contained within.

Cover and Interior Design: Joanna Dion Brown Graphic Design
Publisher: Shamashi Press
Editor: Dawn Raffel
Library of Congress Catalog Number: 2016907868
ISBN: 978-0-692-71355-6.
1. Religion: Judaism–Rituals & Practice 2. Self–Help: Death, Grief & Bereavement 3. Social Science: Jewish Studies
First Edition 10 9 8 7 6 5 4 3 2 1

PRESENTED TO

_____

BY

_____

IN LOVING MEMORY OF

_____

ON

_____

To my Son,

JONAH

May God make you like Ephraim and Menashe
May God bless you and watch over you
May God shine His face on you and show you favor
May God be favorably disposed toward you,

And may He grant you peace.

– GENESIS 48:20

I should like to call attention to the following facts. During the past thirty years, people from all civilized countries of earth have consulted me. I have treated many hundreds of patients.... Protestants...Jews (and a small number of Catholics). Among all my patients...there has not been one whose problem in the last resort was not the finding of a religious outlook on life. It is safe to say that every one of them fell ill because he had lost that which the living religions of every age have given to their followers, and none of them has really been healed who did not have a religious outlook on life.

-CARL JUNG

CONTENTS

PROLOGUE

The Soul Slowly Seeps Out

My entire childhood, my parents staunchly refused to let any of us to have an animal in the house, particularly a dog, and I really wanted a dog. My siblings were much older than I. They moved out when I was young and I grew up as an only child. I needed company. So as a gift when I was eight years old, my brother Gideon broke the house rule and brought home a cute and rambunctious blond mutt that I named Ashi. I had no idea how to care for little Ashi or how to housebreak him. My brother returned to university and I was left with an untrained dog. That did not last long, especially when Ashi peed and pooped all over the house, particularly on my parents' expensive Persian carpets. My mother quickly demanded that Gideon return home and remove this dog. Gideon found a new home for Ashi and I never saw him again.

Many years later, well into my adult married life, when my father was dying of cancer, he finally shared with us that he did like dogs, but had hid that fact from us to avoid the responsibility of taking care of one. When I adopted my cocker spaniel after my marriage, my dad came clean about his own childhood pet dog, Ursik. I think the name I chose,

Ashi, a Persian-sounding name that I had never heard before, was just as comical as Ursik. I can only imagine that somehow my dad and I were subliminally connected through the funny names we chose for our dogs—I was linked to my Dad in more ways than I realized. It was sweet, I thought, and it humanized my dad for me. As my father was slowly dying, he would easily share his life stories with me. There were no filters between his ego and thoughts; he just let everything flow. On the one hand, I felt like it was his way of making peace with himself and with me, and on the other it was if he wanted me to be a witness to his life. He wanted me to remember, cherish and learn his life so that I could share it.

This was a far contrast from the man I knew when I was growing up, whom I viewed as a stuffed shirt. My father was an emotionally distant man, who wore only suits (even on Sundays!) and seemed to view his children as a fulfillment of duties to be fruitful and multiply. My siblings and I felt like we were born for the family portrait. Behind the facade was terrible dysfunction.

My relationship with my father in my formative years was nearly non-existent. He was the patriarch, a mover and shaker in the illustrious gemstone business with offices worldwide, and a benefactor to many Jewish organizations. This led him to live six months of the year in New York and the remaining six months in Thailand. Being raised in a traditional, loud Sephardi home where entertaining family and guests was the norm, I felt like part of the landscape— lost to the opulent background of grand marble halls and spiral staircase. Since I was the last child of four and there was a large age difference between me and my older siblings, I did not have any toys to play with. My parents had given them all away and were not interested in starting over again. I was left to my own devices to self-entertain. A typical example of this is the one time I took a cardboard box and cut out windows and a door to make a dollhouse. I used the leftover cardboard to carve out the furniture and family for the dollhouse, while drawing in the rest of the details. I was usually left in a corner by myself with little interaction. I don't regret any of this today, because I believe these solo experiences cultivated my creativity, but at the time I did feel very neglected.

I grew closer to my father when he developed multiple myeloma, a cancer of the white blood cells that eats away at the bones. I watched him living in tremendous pain, regularly taking oxycodone. As the disease progressed, like the main character from the movie Benjamin Button, he became infantilized due to his lack of independence. Something about his vulnerability and his suffering made me see him as a sweet old man, not the father who was too busy to show up for my high school graduation.

As my father spiraled toward death, he shared more of himself, his childhood in Afghanistan and Pakistan, his married life to my mother in India, and his business life in Thailand. The filters of his thoughts were lifting. The line between consciousness and unconsciousness were blurred. There was something very poignant about this for me. I knew he was dying: He was in hospice and had outlived his doctor's prediction of three to nine more months. I felt that this slow, steady seeping out of the soul was a natural process. It was God's way of easing my father, and us, into the transition of his death, rather than having it come as an abrupt shock.

A few months prior to his passing, he was lying in agony on the living room sofa. My mother gave him morphine for the pain, but probably too little to help. My father's bones were fragile, and he also suffered terrible tooth pain. He explained that it was a shooting pain that gashed at him to the point where he could not talk. His agony compelled me to do something more than morphine. I ran out to the drug store, purchased a heat pack and applied it to his cheek as I massaged his hands. He perked up a bit and said that he was feeling relieved. Within minutes he fell asleep. This process showed me how in times of deep pain and despair we need tender, loving care. Somehow, being a part of my fathers' pain and relief redeemed him of all the sadness and disappointment I felt at not having him around in my formative years.

Reflections on my father's Death

My father passed away on the 9th of August, 2014, at his home in New York (13 Av, 5774, in the Jewish calendar; this is the date we memorialize his death every year). He fought multiple myeloma bravely and with dignity, and rarely complained about his pain or his impending death. When my sister reached me in London, where I was traveling, to let me know that my father had died, my initial reaction was shock. That was followed by centering myself to make burial arrangements and to write the eulogy. Although I was in a mental fog, focusing on the burial arrangements felt like I was in a safe container, shielded from the outside world. The next phase was the intense, week-long process of "sitting" shiva, first with only family and then with our comforting visitors. Having them surround me was like a warm embrace. At 30 days, we entered a new phase of the grieving process, and the frame widened with more activities I could participate in—for one; I could cut my unruly hair, an activity that had been off-limits in the immediate aftermath of the death. My family and I arranged to have a large dinner gathering in a hall and memorialize my father with stories and prayers. At the end of the year-long mourning process, we organized my father's death anniversary (yahrtzeit), in Israel at his graveside with my family members and first cousins from my father's side.

The process of mourning throughout the year was systematic; intense at first and then gradually easing. Every year at the death anniversary, we hold a special commemoration for my father, gathering friends and family for a meal, lighting a candle, reciting The Mourners Prayer and donating to charity.

I know that my father mourned for his own parents in the most complete way he could. While he did sit the week of intense mourning (shiva), observed the customary 30 days, and even recited The Mourners Prayer for his parents for 11 months[1], he also attended festive parties, which is typically avoided for the year. He probably would not have minded if I had gone to parties during the year of mourning, as he would not have wanted me to miss out on family festivities. Family gatherings meant everything to him. Although he was an absentee father, when it came to family celebrations, he would fly in for them from anywhere in the world.

I decided to opt out of all parties that had live music for the year and follow the traditional way of mourning. Whenever there was a festive event that I could not attend (and there were many that year), that was the time when I had to confront the mourning. I felt separated, quarantined from everyone else, and while it was not pleasant, it was necessary. I knew that my isolation was not designed be a punishment, but more like a "time out" to reflect on how my dad could not participate. We were both consoling each other at a psycho-spiritual level. Through the confinement, I connected and reflected. The time-bound Jewish way of mourning, with all its psychological insight, created a means for me to carry my father within throughout the journey. The laws of mourning freed me from social norms and expectations, allowing me to focus on memories of my father, in order to move forward in life in the most meaningful and holistic way possible.

---

1   Shulchan Aruch, Yoreh Deah 376:4. The rabbinic 12 months of mourning is actually 12 months; however, *kaddish* is said for 11 months.

One of those ways was through writing. It is a wonderful companion to a loss, when we feel alone. Writing this book has been cathartic. It has clarified my thoughts and deepened my appreciation of the process of mourning.

I share these Jewish ritualistic pearls of wisdom with you, along with my own journey, because they are the birthright of every Jew, no matter what your Jewish affiliation. Even if you are picking up this book and perusing it after the death, there is still a wealth of benefit embedded in these Jewish traditions. I share with you the necessity of mourning.

DAHLIA ABRAHAM-KLEIN

January 2016–Tevet 5776

Great Neck, New York

PREFACE

JEWISH FUNERALS have vastly changed throughout the millennia. In the past, when a Jew died in the community, The Jewish Burial Society (*Chevra Kaddisha*) just appeared and prepared the body for burial. This was at a time when Jews predominately lived among themselves, and any news was community news. The bereaved family barely needed to make decisions, as most people knew what to do—everyone showed up for the burial and attended to the grieving family. Jews knew how to "do death" and how to comfort the bereaved simply by being ensconced in Jewish life.

With the onset of industrialization, community and families dispersed. Since there is less of a Jewish communal life, our traditional rituals have been replaced with secular burial customs, adopting secular attitudes. Many Jews don't recognize that there is a wealth of tradition to help us through the grieving process, and that it's readily available to all of us, even those who didn't grow up in religious households.

I believe one of the biggest obstacles that many Jews face is the perception that "it's all or nothing." If you are unaffiliated, perhaps you didn't grow up in an observant household or something limited your practice or changed your view. If you didn't grow up with these traditions, some of them might feel "ill fitting"—as in foreign. Perhaps you've never seen a family member mourn in this way or it's just not part of your family history. Since Judaism is such a family-centered religion, I understand how some people might hesitate, feeling unwelcome or not entitled if they don't have a family willing or able to participate with them. It's important to understand that there are many different points of entry for Jewish mourning—and many synagogues will welcome mourners with open arms. There is great psychological, spiritual and emotional benefit to doing what you can. No one does everything to the exact letter of the law.

Unfortunately, secular life offers little in the way of consolation and structure. We live in a culture that is *death defying*. You can see it in the suppression of feelings with overly prescribed anti-depressants; plastic surgery to erase the signs of age; elderly people in nursing homes, tucked out of site from their families; cushioned coffins that seem as if the deceased is having a long sleep while dressed in formal attire, and gatherings after a funeral that seem more like cocktail parties. The bottom line is that we find ourselves in a society that has conditioned us to suppress grief and sorrow and try to create an artificial, plasticized youth.

I have found that the Jewish way of mourning plumbs you right into the reality of death, deeply and intensely. It allows you to *feel* your loss, so that you can move on in the most meaningful way possible.

I approached Jewish mourning as a buffet—I took what inspired me, although I did try to stretch myself. I reached, and in return the process *reached* me.

What is Death?

Death is almost a taboo topic, since we are hardwired to gravitate toward pleasure. It's only natural since pleasure is a survival skill. Who wants to deal with the inevitable finality of death? The Jewish definition of death is best presented by first asking: What is life?

There is a Jewish idea of life, as the fusion of soul and body, where the body is the vehicle for the soul's expression. The soul is absolutely pure, and the challenge in life is for the soul—the navigator—to drive the vehicle to its highest potential, bringing divinity to this world.

The word for dead in Hebrew is *niftar*. It also means to be released from duty—to be summoned back after service. The multiple meanings for the word *niftar* imply that this world is the world of work. You can use your physical body to elevate this world through good deeds. When the body has shut down, it has completed its job in this world and gets summoned back to Source.

Death dissolves the body and soul into two separate entities—the spiritual self and the vehicle for that self. The self is the soul, not the body. Just as thoughts are invisible, feelings are invisible: We can't see them but we know they are there. This life of the body is just a vestibule—one phase—though a most important phase, of its existence—an existence, which precedes physical life and extends beyond it.

A metaphoric way of describing this phenomenon in scientific and spiritual terms is through Albert Einstein's prodigious scientific equation, $E=mc^2$. It represents the correlation of energy to matter: Essentially, energy and matter are interchangeable. Both energy and matter might appear as two separate entities, but it is one reality that just takes on different shapes and forms—the energy is not destroyed, just transformed. In simple terms, with the decomposition of the body (mass)—the transformation from one state to another—the *soul* (energy) is released. Death is simply a means of travel to another source. Although we can't *see* it, our loved ones' *memory* is eternal.

We can never fully grasp the concept of the soul and the impact it has had in this world, but the connection between us and our loved ones lives on. Our Jewish sages state that the soul of the person we knew and loved as a physical being on this earth continues to exist after death, continues to be aware of all that transpires in our lives, and continues to be the recipient of our love and the positive actions *we* do on his behalf.[1]

A fundamental principle of the Jewish faith is the belief in "resurrection of the dead." In the Messianic vision of the "World to Come," the soul will be restored to a rebuilt and revitalized body. The body is a vehicle from God that is on loan. We must return it as He gave it. That is why we don't

---

1   Berachos 18b.

desecrate the body in any form after the body has served its duty.

This understanding of the soul underlies the Jewish approach to death and mourning. The many customs, beliefs and mystical motifs related to death—its prequel and sequel, the treatment of the deceased, the approach to mourning, and the ways in which the beloved is memorialized—are driven by a series of Jewish rituals.

Jewish Ritual

Rituals hold a central place in Judaism. For me, they helped to legitimize my personal feelings in my time of grief. They built a protective fence that enabled me to heal. They kept me within reasonable bounds, offering specific benchmarks for my grief—base points that ushered me through the mourning process. Ritual also guided me as to how much or how little to memorialize my father, helping me to avoid the extremes of pathology and denial.

Even Sigmund Freud, the grandfather of modern psychology, suggested that small acts of ritual could mold a mourner's thinking and create mental health.[2] Rituals, like all habit-forming actions, subtly rewire the brain. With repetition, that rewiring creates the impetus for change and even transcendence—the ability to rise out of an ordinary experience into a transformative one.

---

2   Sigmund Freud, Mourning and Melancholia (1917).

The Five Stages to Mourning

Jewish ritual offers a practical and contained pathway to the physical, psychological and spiritual directives of mourning. This beautiful, structured approach involves five concentric circles that spiral open to wider circles of opportunity.

1. Deep despair (*oh-nein*). The first, most intense circle of mourning is the period between the death and the burial. It enfolds the first-degree relatives (parent, sibling, spouse or child), consuming their energy with the funeral and burial arrangements.

2. Seven days of intense mourning. After the burial, first-degree relatives sit *shiva* for one week.

3. The 30-day period following burial (*shloshim*). In this stage, the mourner reenters the world by leaving the shiva house and going back to work. The prescribed mourning practices end unless they have lost a parent.

4. The first year (*ah-vel*). This is the prescribed time frame for mourning a parent. Within the year, a special memorial takes place and the headstone is unveiled, a memorial candle is lit and family gathers.

5. The death anniversary (*yahrtzeit*). Every year, on the Jewish date of death, we remember and memorialize the life and accomplishments of the beloved.

These five stages helped to guide me through loss and gradually ease me back into the world. The loss is forever, but the psychological, emotional and spiritual healing that took place at every stage was necessary and healthy.

In the infancy of mourning, the initial shock we feel can be compared to that of a newborn who has entered the world. While the newborn is unaware and afraid of its surroundings, and has no idea what life has in store, we the onlookers know that the newborn will go through necessary stages of growth in that first year—earmarks for development. The same holds true for the mourner. There are contained and structured milestones for growth. Each stage opens the door to a wider world and a broader understanding. I understand this now, long after the yearlong process of mourning, as I have the benefit of hindsight.

Years before Robert Frost's famous quip, "The best way out is always through," the Jewish sages understood that the mourner needed that time to grieve, to *actively* participate and reflect on the mourning process. There is something psychologically profound about this choreography of mourning. It was not just to honor the memory of my father, but also to honor the loss, find meaning in it and carry on in life in the most complete way possible.

The Case for Mourning

Why mourn? I believe there are three profound reasons. First, to sanctify the life of the deceased. If death is cheap, then life is cheap. Second, those who mourn well, live well. Third, mourning is the healing process of the heart, soul and mind; it is the path that returns us to wholeness.

When mourning is done mindfully, the bereaved have a better chance of making healthy decisions that are not governed by unmetabolized grief and pain. These beautiful rituals predates what Sigmund Freud coined as "grief work." He maintained that "working through" our grief is critically important—a process that we neglect at our peril. Grief work involves an active, ongoing effort to come to terms with the death, whereas avoiding the mourning process can lead to neurotic decisions, denial or numbness, outbursts of anger and isolation. Unstructured grief that doesn't progress can lock you into yourself, leaving no room for anyone to console you. Or it can lead you into an inappropriate relationship born out of hunger to replace the deceased.

The Code of Jewish Law (Shulchan Aruch) says, "One should not grieve too much for the dead and whosoever grieves excessively is really grieving for someone else."[3] Rituals provide a healthy boundary for grief.

Unfinished Mourning

These aren't just intellectual ideas. If we don't mourn, grief will find ways of breaking into our lives. Not knowing how to handle the pain of mourning, we avoid it; not realizing

---

3   Code of Jewish Law (Shulchan Aruch), quoted in Jack Riemer, Jewish Reflections on Death (New York: Schocken Books, 1975.), chapter 394.

it is the pain of the loss we are trying to avoid. A pain that will strike, no matter how much we try to avoid it. By avoidance, we turn our backs to the help that mourning offers, prolonging the pain.

Samuel, a charming and excellent salesman, who is also a workaholic, never shared too much personal information with his coworkers. His focus was about making other people feel good, which in part is what made him outstanding at his profession. The flip side was that he did not have any close friends and unbeknown to everyone, he was a loner. When his father died, he went to work as usual as if it was a regular workday, and didn't tell any of his colleagues. He did not want to give off any sense of mourning or that he was falling apart, so he stifled his feelings. Samuel was raised by a strict German father who taught him that "real men" don't cry. Samuel put a lid on the mourning process so he would not have to deal with it.

After work, Samuel just locked up his store and went to bury his father. He never sat through the intense week long mourning (shiva), never recited The Mourning Prayer and did not go back to visit his parents at the cemetery, even though he claims he had a great relationship with them both. Samuel felt that that there was little reason to mourn his parents because he was an excellent son— always helpful to them, be it driving them to their doctor appointments or fixing their television. What Samuel seemed to miss is the importance of mourning for his psychological benefit and for his parent's memory. He did not know that mourning is not solely for grieving, but more importantly, to *sanctify* his parents' lives. The year of mourning is to engrave in your mind and heart your parents' essence. In order to do that, a mourner must focus without distractions. He must honor the life his parents led and the values they transmitted to him. Otherwise, their lives seem weightless.

Samuel was living with his longtime girlfriend in an unloving and uncommunicative relationship. He disclosed to me that he just could not end their relationship, despite the fact that they were estranged. In his mind, his girlfriend was the last connection to his parents. They both liked her, so losing her would mean losing them—a fact he did not process. I pointed this out to him, as well as the fact that, because he did not mourn his parents at all, this had affected his life with ill-considered decisions. His pain festered, and all of a sudden a previous loss resurfaced. With continued encouragement from me to see a therapist, Samuel finally did end that "no love lost" relationship, mourned her and his parents (albeit ten years later) and became more introspective. Unfinished mourning always makes itself known.

Grief and illness

When my friend Linda lost her mother, she too skipped the Jewish ritual process of mourning. For one year, she was terribly depressed, crying at the least provocation. She did not go out at all and had little contact with the outside world, except to go to work. Linda did not belong to a community, and had little support structure. Her grieving was very complicated, not progressing and not contained. Soon after, she became gravely ill. Thankfully, she recovered. While I can't say the two events are correlated, there are several research claims that if grieving does not progress, it has the potential to cause great illness.[4]

If your mourning is not structured (or even if it is) and you feel haggard, help your mind and body recover by doing kind things for them—exercise more, eat better, get to bed earlier and sleep a little later. If you are out of balance, take small steps and pay attention to your mind and body.

While we don't have control of when or if we will fall ill, the Jewish way of mourning, with all its spiritual and psychological insights, is designed to reconnect you to yourself, to draw you into your soul. The focus is away from the temporal, the vulnerable, and back to the Source, which is strong. The soul is the purest part of you, the part that is connected to love, the part that is connected to God, the part that is beyond the body and health and disease.

Grief and Relationships

Extra-marital affairs are more common after a death in the family, because the "high" of the affair—the aliveness—is

---

4   A. Tomarken, J. Holland, S. Schachter, et al., "Factors of complicated grief pre-death in caregivers of cancer patients." Psycho-Oncology volume 17 issue 2 (2008): 105-11.

counter to the dullness of grief.[5] Daniel, an attractive young man had an "ice box" of a mother growing up. He was happily married to a lovely woman. She was very nurturing to him, but she had to travel extensively for work. At his own job, Daniel had a collegial relationship with a female coworker. After his mother passed away, he went through the motions of some of the ritualistic mourning, but past the 30-day marker life went back to "normal." That's when Daniel and his office-mate amped up their relationship. Their boundaries started to melt. She, like his mother, was a bit of an ice queen, but according to Daniel's account, he was the only one who could emotionally warm her up and deeply know her. He felt empowered and alive. Daniel had re-found his mother in this woman, the mother he'd longed to "de-ice" and now he was finally successful.

After death, it feels as if you've hit a wall, and you need to find some softness in your life. For Daniel, death felt like a broken connection and the affair felt like a new beginning. It was not necessarily about sex, but about the closeness that sex made possible.

To this date, Daniel and his paramour are still involved with each another. Daniel has shared with me that he loves his wife, yet has a deep connection to his lover. He's aware of the dichotomy of his feelings, and he's seeing a therapist to become more self-aware and honest about his innate needs.

Perhaps if Daniel had understood the benefits of

5 Esther Perel. "Why Happy Couples Cheat." (TED Talks, May 2015) YouTube Video, 21 min, 30 sec. https://youtu.be/P2AUat93a8Q (Accessed 2/15/16).

mourning at that time, the affair could have been averted. An affair often lives in the shadow of death and mortality, because they raise the questions: Is there more to life? Am I going to continue with this mundane marriage? Will I ever feel alive again? These important inner questions need to be addressed during the mourning process. Otherwise, they can propel people to cross the line into the arms of another to avoid facing the finality of loss.

◆————————▶

Fully immersing yourself in the mourning process in all its stages is, paradoxically, the antidote to death. It forces you to face those existential questions and gives you the space to reflect. The death of a loved one can give your life more meaning, new insights and perhaps a new direction, but all this comes from internal work, not by acting out anxiety. If you avoid the mourning process, the deceased are not honored, not sanctified and not cherished, but rather switched out for another person or ideal.

STAGE ONE

◀━━━━━━━━━━━━━━━━━━▶

Deep Distress

Death is a rupture in the fabric of one's life. It upends everything, creating a sense of dislocation and upheaval. The first stage of mourning may run the gamut of feelings from shock, disbelief and denial to relief and peace. According to Jewish tradition, as soon as you learn of a death, you must stop what you are doing and occupy yourself with the burial process—the focus must be on the deceased. It is the last real gift you can give them. Jewish law constructs a protective fence around mourners at this initial stage. They are exempt from all regular activity: no business, no social gatherings, no required blessings over food, no meat and wine (because they symbolize festivity) and refraining from sexual intimacy.

A Soul Wavering

I WAS IN LONDON on a business trip with my husband when I got a text message from my sister: "Father has passed." I read the text; there was a second of disbelief before I gasped. Then I emotionally collapsed. I felt like I was melting and numb at the same time. It was a twilight experience: not here, not there; not day, not night. I needed air. I needed to move. I needed to run. I walked the streets of London with my husband in complete inner chaos with no destination. I just walked until my legs couldn't carry me any longer. Inside I felt like a had a fever—restless, bizarrely energized and depleted at the same time.

Our Jewish sages state that the soul is in flux until the body is buried in the ground.[1] The soul feels disarrayed, as it is no longer stored in the earthly body. I believe just as my father's soul was wandering at this period of time, I felt a similar state of bewilderment. There was such a surge of flighty energy. I found making burial arrangements held me in a safe capsule for a while.

Interestingly, I vividly remember that when each of my grandparents died, my mother and her sisters would start

1   Shabbos 152b, Sefer Mitzvos Gadol, Esin DeRabanan 2 (Vinitzia, 5307) p. 246a.

baking before the burial. They explained to me that it was tradition to bake a mourner's pastry, called in Bukharian *cushkelik*. This spiral pastry symbolized the cycle of life and the ascent of the soul. The baking centered them and gathered my aunts in unison to talk about their parent.

Writing The Eulogy

After I released my restless energy by walking, I sat down and wrote the eulogy for my father. I could not focus on writing until I had physically exhausted myself. Only then could my stream of thoughts flow. The writing of the eulogy contained me. It preoccupied me; it felt like a safe place to go.

The eulogy allowed me to lament, and bring myself and others to tears. Abraham, the first patriarch of the Jewish people, eulogized his wife Sarah (Genesis 23:2), and that has been the custom of Jews to this day.

The writing helped to impose some kind of order on my chaotic feelings. It put my father's personality and accomplishments into sharp focus. He was a leader within his Jewish community, a benefactor to many Jewish causes, and a mediator. He never over-thought anything. When the Rebbe (Menachem Mendel Schneerson, the last Lubavitcher Rebbe) asked him to build a mikvah (ritual bath) in Bangkok, my father did, although it took 14 years. My father was an eternal optimist and saw life through rose-colored glasses. Writing helped me clearly see the goodness in him and begin the healing processes.

For people who have difficulty writing a eulogy, the clergy or the officiate of the ceremony may be able to help elicit memories. They know how to ask questions that trigger memories and feelings, helping bring comfort and order amid the tumultuous emotions.

The Sanctity of the Deceased Body

My family was actively involved with the body from the time of death to burial. The Jewish sages explain that the body must never be left alone, as the soul is in a state of chaos and pain, being in the midst of two worlds—the earthly world and the spiritual world—until the body is buried.[2]

Since my father died early Sabbath morning, we couldn't prepare for his burial until the Sabbath ended that night. Then we contacted my parents' rabbi, who arranged for my father's body to be picked up by the Jewish Burial Society (*Chevra Kadisha*), who saw to it that the body was prepared for burial according to Jewish tradition.

Watching the Body

After my father took his last labored breath and my mother's wailing subsided, she draped a cloth over his entire body and face. According to Jewish tradition, it's disrespectful for the body to be up on display, as it's considered "humiliation of the dead," a desecration of the

2   Shulchan Aruch, Yoreh Deah 339:3. Babylonian Talmud: Avodah Zarah 20b, Pirkei Rabbi Eliezer.

image of God. She then asked my father's brother and her sisters, who all live close by, to "watch" the body, as it may never be left alone. A general atmosphere of reverence was maintained. Eating, drinking, singing and playing music was completely avoided. According to Judaism, these are physical pleasures the deceased cannot enjoy any longer,[3] so out of respect no one engaged in any of these activities until the Jewish Burial Society collected the body.

Each person in the room was left with quiet time with my father for words of reconciliation that perhaps had not been said in life. Now was the time to ask forgiveness for causing any pain or sadness. My sister Shirley held my dad's hand, kissed it and said she felt at peace.

When my father's body was picked up by the Jewish Burial Society (Chevra Kadisha) and prepared for burial, his body was never left alone. A guardian (shomer) was hired to stay with the body at all times. According to rabbinic legend (midrash), the human soul is somewhat lost and confused between death and before burial, and it stays in the general vicinity of the body, until the body is interred.[4] The guardian sits and reads aloud psalms during the time that they are watching the body. This serves as a comfort to the spirit of the departed who is in transition.

---

3   This is alluded to in the verse (Job 14:22), "And his soul mourns for him."

4   Genesis Rabbah 100:7 and Leviticus Rabbah 18:1.

Psalms of Comfort

The recitation of psalms—Jewish sacred songs or hymns—in times of distress, uncertainty and thanksgiving provides comfort, as they reflect a personal relationship with God. There are 150 psalms whose authorship is attributed to King David (10th century B.C.E.), and they are the most famous of all religious poetry. Some are recited every day, and others are particularly relevant in a time of death. My uncle Samuel, seated by my father's side, recited Psalm 23 ("The Lord is my Shepherd") and Psalm 91, which speaks of God as Protector and refuge. All throughout the Sabbath, my father's little brother Samuel sat by the body and prayed to God, with the psalms found below, that his brother's soul would be comforted. Uncle Samuel had always been protected by my father. Now the roles were reversed.

Psalm 23

A song of David. The Lord is my shepherd; I shall not want. He causes me to lie down in green pastures; He leads me beside still waters. He restores my soul; He leads me in paths of righteousness for His name's sake. Even when I walk in the valley of darkness, I will fear no evil for You are with me; Your rod and our staff—they comfort me. You set a table before me in the presence of my adversaries; You anointed my head with oil; my cup overflows. May only goodness and kindness pursue me all the days of my life, and I will dwell in the house of the Lord for long days.

Psalm 91

You who dwell in the shelter of the Most High, who abide in the shadow of the Omnipotent: I say of the Lord who is my refuge and my stronghold, my God in whom I trust, that He will save you from the ensnaring trap, from the destructive pestilence. He will cover you with His pinions and you will find refuge under His wings; His truth is a shield and an armor. You will not fear the terror of the night, nor the arrow that flies by day; the pestilence that prowls in the darkness, nor the destruction that ravages at noon. A thousand may fall at your [left] side, and ten thousand at your right, but it shall not reach you. You need only look with your eyes, and you will see the retribution of the wicked. Because you [have said,] "The Lord is my shelter," and you have made the Most High your haven, no evil will befall you, no plague will come near your tent. For He will instruct His angels on your behalf, to guard you in all your ways. They will carry you in their hands, lest you injure your foot upon a rock. You will tread upon the lion and the viper; you will trample upon the young lion and the serpent. Because he desires Me, I will deliver him; I will fortify him, for he knows My Name. When he calls on Me, I will answer him; I am with him in distress. I will deliver him and honor him. I will satiate him with long life, and show him My deliverance.

STAGE ONE *Deep Distress*

Expediting the Burial

Traditionally, burial occurs within the day, a custom based on the line in the Torah: "You shall bury him the same day.... His body should not remain all night" (Deuteronomy 21:23). There are some exceptions to delaying the burial, such as when the body needs to be transported or when family members need to travel to the funeral. Among all my siblings, only my sister was in New York when my father passed away. Gideon was in Thailand with his kids and my son; Jackie, my other brother, was with his family in Miami; and I was in London. The burial was to take place in Israel. We all had to make speedy arrangements to fly to Israel.

The psychological benefit to be derived from following the tradition is that it becomes a matter of almost unbearable mental strain for us to " walk in the valley of darkness" for an extended amount of time. No one deserves to be subjected to the despair and anguish of being continually in the physical company of the body, no matter how deep their affection. As it is spiritually proper for the body to be buried without delay, so it is emotionally advisable for the family not to have to undergo the pain of an unduly long wait.

Preparing the Body for Burial

Jewish law is explicit in its details of caring for the body, since the human body is seen as the image of God even when the soul has departed. This accounts for many of the detailed practices regarding burial, and why we bury our dead rather than destroying the "image of God." Burning the body is seen as a desecration of what once was holy. For some Jews who find that it's not easy making decisions about the disposing of the body, the parameters of Jewish tradition ease the disorientation by connecting the decisions to Jewish rituals. The duty is upon the community as a whole to care for their members, through the help of the *Chevra Kadisha*.

A friend of mine was involved with the Chevra Kadisha in the community she grew up in. She would perform the ritual washing and preparation of the body for burial (tahara). Washing a dead body might sound morbid, but it was an incredibly spiritual and meaningful experience for her. There was so much respect for the body of a stranger, so much care given. She shared that it was comforting to see that any member of the community would be cared for all the way until the end, regardless of whether they had family or means. Sometimes, depending on which hospital the body came from, the hands and feet would be tied with zip ties, trussed—it reminded her of a chicken. It felt like a tremendous lack of respect. This was now just a body, just something to be removed and dealt with, tied up and wrapped in plastic, which stood out so starkly against the way Jewish ritual treats the body. In fact, there is a prohibition against passing an object over the dead body, which just affirms the humanity of the person whose body is lying there. Jewish tradition ensures that the Chevra Kadisha continue to accord a dead person the respect given to those still alive—dignity, respect and care are always provided for the person this body had been.

After the ritual washing (mikvah), the body is dried off. Then the face and body are covered and draped with a natural linen shroud. The shroud has no pockets, so neither wealth nor status can be conveyed in the attire. Interestingly, when a baby is born we bathe and wrap the newborn in swaddling clothes. Death completes the cycle of life.

As the newborn progresses through the stages into adulthood, living a material life, he wastes so much of his life keeping up with others and trying to get ahead. He becomes so envious of what the other person has that he can't enjoy what he has. He becomes self involved in a frantic hamster-in-a-wheel race to do more, to have more, to be more. In the end, the messages of death, and the Jewish tradition to be buried in simple linen shrouds, teach us a lesson for life. We leave this world in human equality and what we leave behind are our good deeds. That's it.

The Funeral

A funeral typically takes place in the synagogue, funeral home, cemetery chapel or by the grave. Jewish ritual requires a closed coffin as another step in affirming the finality of death. Furthermore, Jewish tradition is sensitive to the dignity of the deceased. The body can no longer function and no longer see, yet we can *see* the body. When we look at the body, it becomes a spectacle, an object, which is antithetical to the sanctity of the body. The closed coffin forces family members to begin thinking about the person as a memory, which begins the separation process.

My father's funeral service was at the synagogue he helped found in Queens, New York, more than 40 years ago. How poignant, since this synagogue was a place of life cycle events for my father. He was president for many years, then treasurer for many years, and served innumerable functions within his community. Many family celebrations were held there, including the Shabbat Chattan, when my husband-to-be was called to the Torah the Sabbath before our wedding. My son's bris was carried out there as well. Now the synagogue was the place to memorialize my father's death. Life had come full circle.

The Hebrew word for funeral is levaya, which means accompanying. The same way we accompany our loved ones through the journeys that are their lives, Jewish tradition teaches us how we may journey with them to their final rest, and beyond. It was incumbent upon my mother and sister, who were in New York for the funeral service (while I was in London), to provide my father a dignified departure within the support of the community.

My sister shared with me that when services were done, the pallbearers carried the body to the hearse. The hearse drove slowly while all attendants accompanied the body, walking behind it as a final farewell. The cars of family and friends, with their headlights on and hazard lights flashing, followed the hearse to the airport hangar.

Whenever I see a school of cars with flashing lights driving along the highway, there is always a solemnness that comes over me. Someone has died, a family is grieving. It's a call for the public to stop and share in the sorrow, no matter who it is. A life has ended. Private loss compels public notice, as it has from time immemorial.

The Burial

Rending of the Garments (K'riah)

Jewish tradition prescribes that first-degree relatives (children, siblings, spouse and parents) are to express their pain and sorrow by tearing their clothes (when mourning a parent, one tears on the left side. For all others, one tears on the right side).[5] How psychologically sound that Judaism provides a safe physical opportunity for psychological relief. A mourner can vent his pent-up anguish by means of a controlled, religiously sanctioned act of destruction. This is usually done at the beginning of the funeral service. (Alternatively, some communities perform the rending

---

5   The Torah records many instances of rending the clothes after the news of death. When Jacob saw Joseph's coat of many colors drenched with what he thought to be his son's blood, he rent his garments. Likewise, David tore his clothes when he heard of the death of King Saul, and Job, who knew grief so well, stood up and rent his mantle.

immediately following the death, or upon the interment in the grave.)

For my father's death, the rending was done at the burial site in a separate room where my father's body was covered in a shroud, laid out on a table awaiting burial. I was wearing a heather grey jersey dress with a black lace collar. The officiating rabbi handed my cousin Yochevet what looked like a surgical knife. She made the initial cut on my dress at the left side of my chest over my heart.[6] It carried so much drama. I lifted my hands and tore it further open. That tear was an expression, an opening to release the feelings in my heart. The tearing was a rending of my relationship with my father. We were torn apart. We all felt a pang, as if that initial cut was a tear into our flesh.

The tearing of my pretty dress carried multiple meanings for me. The dress I was wearing, this material object, was not real. It was real in the sense that I could see it and touch it, but at the end of the day the attractive dress was just a material, fleeting item. It could be replaced. My father could not be replaced. The loss of an article of clothing graphically symbolized the personal sense of loss. It's customary to invoke a common Jewish blessing before the rending: Baruch Dayan Ha'Emet, "Blessed is the True Judge" in English. It might sound like an odd blessing to say in times of loss and tragedy, but it's tradition. With these words, I am acknowledging that this is the Truth. In

---

6   According to Jewish ritual, that the rending for a parent is on the left side of the chest, to "expose the heart" (that is, that the tear for deceased parents must be over the heart), indicates that the tear in the apparel represents a torn heart.

this way, I help myself move into acceptance, rather than denial. Even events that seem bad are all meant to be part of the natural cycle of life and death, as God is the True Judge. I responded with "Amen."

Gravesite

According to Jewish law, the body should return to the earth, the source of all physical life, and be reunited with it, so the soul can travel to its next destination (olam haba).[7] The natural decomposition of the body into the earth allows the expeditious return of the soul to its Source. Therefore, it is custom to bury in a simple pine coffin, because it erodes quickly. Another reason for the simple casket is the great Jewish symbol of equality in death—we all leave this world in the same manner we entered, with no status.[8]

---

7   According to our Jewish sages, the actions of the person themselves constitute the reward in Olam Haba. After the soul departs from the body it rises to take pleasure and satisfaction with the light, energy and worlds of Holiness that have been added and multiplied by his good actions.

8   According to the Babylonian Talmud, Rabbi Gamliel in the 1st century CE established the principle of equality and economy in death. Confronting the excesses of their time, the Jewish sages noted that "the poor were shamed" by practices that highlighted socioeconomic inequalities in death. These included viewing the faces of the deceased rich while covering the famine-disfigured faces of the deceased poor, and displaying the deceased rich on an ornamented couch while the deceased poor were brought out for burial on a plain bier. At first, burial of the dead was, for their relatives, more difficult than their death [because of the expense], to the point at which relatives would leave their dead and flee, as the Talmud describes it. The sages decreed that the faces of all deceased should be covered, and that all should be brought out on a plain bier — "for the honor of the poor."

My father was buried without a coffin, as is often done in Israel.[9] We placed my father's prayer shawl (tallit) on his body. Before the prayer shawl was placed on the body, the rabbi rendered it unfit for use to demonstrate that my father was no longer bound by the religious obligation of the living. There were constant physical reminders of the loss.

The Jewish Burial Society handed us shovels. There were about 25 of us around the open grave—my first cousins, my siblings and my dad's sister. Every person at the gravesite shoveled earth to bury my father. The shovel was not handed from one person to the next; rather each one took up the shovel and put it down again on the Jewish basis that misery should not be passed around.[10] There was no gravedigger to finish the job for us; we all participated in enclosing my father back into this earthly womb. The grave was closed. My dad was really gone.

Ideally, fellow Jews should fill in the whole grave by hand. Where this is not possible, the coffin should at least be completely covered with earth. This ritual helps the bereaved to fully comprehend that the death occurred and allows for the grieving process to truly begin. If there was ever any denial about the death, throwing earth on the deceased is a wake up call that this person is now beginning his journey into the next world (olam haba).

---

9   Abraham and Sarah, the first Jews, were buried without coffins.

10   Samuel Heilman, When a Jew Dies (Berkeley: University of California Press, 2001), 112.

I know this from my own experience. Burying my father was an incredibly difficult and surreal act. My eyes saw the earth slowly swallow him up. The traditions and customs of participating in the burial were psychologically beneficial. The act of shoveling earth onto the body helped to provide a psychological closure by saying goodbye one final time.

STAGE TWO

•——————————•

*The Seven Days
of Intense Mourning*

Jewish tradition guides mourners to sit together for seven days in an intense mourning where the bereaved sit low, known as shiva. Shiva is from the word sheva, which means seven. The number seven in Judaism is very significant, for it symbolizes completion in this world, as in the seven days of creation. Ideally, all of the direct mourners sit shiva in the house of the deceased, as the Jewish sages have stated, "Where a person lived there does his spirit continue to dwell." The presence of the person who has passed away is strongest in his own home, as memories will come easily there, and part of the comfort of the week of shiva is sharing such memories. To accommodate multiple families who live some distance apart, the "sitting" may be moved from one member's house to another.

Arranging the Shiva House

It's not enough to feel the death—your surroundings must match the solemnity of the death as well. The physical set-up of the Shiva house emulates that emotional process. It is customary for friends and family (alternatively, the funeral home, or Jewish Burial Society) to set up the house before the return from the gravesite so that family members don't have to deal with it. Setup includes the following:

Memorial Candle

A memorial candle is lit in the Shiva house, and it remains burning publicly 24 hours per day throughout the entire week. For me, gazing at the candle was a gentle reminder that my dad's memory would be eternal, and helped to bring light into the darkness in which I was immersed.

Our Jewish sages say that a person's soul is compared to a flame, since each person brings light into the world. And just as one can use one flame to light more candles without diminishing the original flame, so too a person can give of himself, touching many lives, without ever being diminished. That light would be internalized within me and never burn out because I could carry my father within me and share his gifts in this world.

Low Stools

The Jewish Burial Society provided chairs for us for the week of shiva. They were wooden, slatted, low-back chairs. They were not comfortable chairs at all. For me, this carried multiple levels of meaning. For one, the focus was not on my physical comfort. Secondly, sitting closer to earth was a way to symbolically connect with my father, who was in the belly of earth. It was a slow physical separation from my dad. There was also the feeling that I was not at the same high-charged emotional level as everyone else at that time—I was solemn. Sitting in that position, which was out of the ordinary, stimulated contemplation, rethinking and stories—many stories flowed.

Mirrors

All mirrors were covered with sheets in the Shiva house, as we were striving to ignore our own physicality and vanity in order to concentrate on the reality of the loss. Not viewing myself in the mirror made me feel invisible, in a sense. It forced me to focus inward, to the reality of my soul and to the loss.

Unlocked Front Door

Typically, the front door is left unlocked and slightly ajar so that visitors can enter without knocking or ringing the doorbell. Since this is the time for solemnness, it is also not the time to be a host. Getting up and opening the door for visitors is a distraction for the mourner.

Photograph of Beloved

My mother brought a large photo of my father to be placed next to the memorial candle. Next to the candle, it seemed as if my father was glowing. The mementos or photos are a way to make it easier to enter the process of remembering.

Meals at the Shiva House

The Meal of Consolation

The first thing we did upon entering the *Shiva* house was sit down to a "meal of condolence"[1] prepared by family and friends. They came to the house before we even returned from the cemetery, and by their presence made us realize that we were not alone. There was something so inherently beautiful in the way the community united to feed us.

This first meal included bread, considered the sustenance of life; and hard-boiled eggs—a food that is round, like the cycle of life. The hard-boiled egg and sometimes lentils (eaten by some Sephardim) carry a symbolic allusion; both egg and lentil have no stem. They are smooth surfaces; they have no opening, no closing, no mouth to speak. There are many different customs relating

---

1   Mishnah Mo'ed Katan 3:7. It is called *seudat havra'ah; meal of health.*

to the symbolic foods eaten. The meal was eaten silently, and the egg reminded us of the silence—no words could describe the grieving heart at that moment.

I believe the deeper psychological reason a mourner must be accommodated with food when they enter the Shiva house is to affirm life, and to live. Furthermore, eating reengages the mourner. It is an act of support for the mourners—the community rescues them, in a sense, from starving themselves and plunging into the earth to follow the deceased. Food is sustenance to the body that retains the soul. Eating grounds us, and that is crucial at a period of time when we feel like we are floating.

The Mourner is not the Host

Even though I was sitting shiva in a foreign country, for the remainder of the week, friends and family brought and sent meals. My sister-in-law, Johana, and my niece, Daniela, flew in from Miami, and every day before the crack of dawn, no matter how bleary-eyed and exhausted, they came to the Shiva house and prepared breakfast for all of us. As a mourner, you are not supposed to serve yourself. It's the same idea as sick people not cooking for themselves, but rather allowing a friend or family member to take care of them during a difficult time. The mourner should think of himself as a guest in his own home. For a self-sufficient person like me, this was a lesson in the need to sometimes rely on others. We are a link in a chain, holding each other in place. The constant care and doting from the community, friends and family was tremendously comforting, and reminded us that we were not alone. Whenever there is pain, it's always lessened by the love, concern and comfort of people who are simply there for you.

At my synagogue in New York, there is a consolation committee—a group of volunteers who reach out to families at a time of loss to help them deal with the myriad practical details of setting up and running a Shiva house. If the family is interested, shiva coordinators are appointed to coordinate meals and other assistance, which is donated by community members. You might find that your synagogue has a similar committee.

This is strikingly different from some of the shivas I have seen among secular Jews. I recall a shiva for my friend Chelsea's mother. Her mother died at the very ripe old age of 102! Chelsea had an ambivalent relationship with her mother, and had bitterly complained about her mother's narcissism for years prior to her death. When her mother died, she sat for the week, but it was a festive catered banquet with live classical music—a kind of "sad party." It reminded me of the movie scene in Titanic where the captain of the ship orders the orchestra to play at the top deck, to avoid panic as the ship was sinking.

Rather than having visitors comfort her, Chelsea was scurrying around making sure we were all comfortable and finding the food at the dining table. It was a thank-you party for attending the shiva. I believe Chelsea did not want to burden the visitors or herself, and was camouflaging her grief by over-emphasizing the long life her mother had led, muffling the loss with music. In my mind, Chelsea's strained and worried face did not match her "hostess with the mostest" demeanor.

Even among the Orthodox, there is a risk of becoming subsumed by a feeling of social obligation. There was a profound reason my mother wanted us to sit shiva in Israel rather than New York, where most of my family, business associates and friends were located. Since my mother is the matriarch of the family, she knew that there would be hundreds of people coming to console us at shiva. She also felt that they would be expecting meals, noshes and drinks, and she would not be able to sit shiva in a mindful manner. People would be darting around her kitchen, asking her where the cups were or where the plates were, and she knew she would not be able to sit still. I believe she made the right decision for us to sit shiva away from all this. The family honored her feelings. She needed to mourn with just a few relatives and she created an appropriate tone.

The shiva is the only time when family and friends are there to share sorrow with you. This is the time when they will openly and tenderly share their love for you. After the week, grieving is mostly solitary. So this is the time to leave the role of host and mourn with those who want to console you. Be present, and give yourself permission to mourn.

Dressing and Living the Week

Work

For Jewish mourners, the ritual is not to leave the Shiva house at any time and not to attend to any work. It's for others to take care of errands or outside commitments for us. Work and productivity are equated as living a full life with maximum output. This is not the week to focus on productivity, but rather inactivity, which reflects lifelessness. I wasn't lifeless, but I was focused on the "lifelessness" of my father. Physical inactivity led to soul searching.

Grooming

The laws of mourning focus on one's spirituality. We de-emphasized our own physicality by not pampering our bodies, to focus on the *essence* of who my father was. During the week I was not supposed to wear makeup, bathe, cut my nails and hair or change clothes. Although I was not supposed to bathe, I did. But rather than take a hot long shower, like I usually do, I bathed in tepid water as a physical reminder that I was in mourning.

Shoes

Leather is a sign of luxury, so I wore nylon sneakers for the week.

Sexual Relations

Sex is a part of life, and it's also part of mourning—that is, the absence of it. Sex represents carnal pleasure and "aliveness." Of course, there is nothing wrong with that; but it has its time. During the shiva week, the focus is inward, not on one's temporal body. Some mourners might feel "covered in death." They think they need to feel the intensity of life, and that sex is the only way to get there. Sex becomes driven by grief. Jewish wisdom reminds us that this prolongs the mourning process, and doesn't give sanctity to the deceased, in the sense that sex is celebrating in the face of their death rather than mourning.

The Sitting Week

The term "sitting shiva" is by design a metaphor for stillness. In the stillness, you are contemplating, thinking and meditating. Sitting is the antonym to standing—as if ready to move forward. Sitting is seated in the reality of the death, and sitting in the silence of it. This is the week to feel the intensity, where you can't run, but sit, dwelling together with friends and loved ones as they come to comfort you with short visits.

Silence

According to Jewish tradition, the first three days of the intense week of mourning are for weeping and silence *without* the presence of comforters. I think there is something incredibly wise about this, although most mourners are not afforded the opportunity to sit silently alone. Usually, when I have gone on "shiva calls" I find that I am in a solemn mood, preparing to mimic the mourner's internal feelings. But really when I greet someone this way, I am imposing my perspective of what the mourner is feeling, and not giving the mourner the opportunity to truly express their own feelings. Sometimes, as for my friends Samuel or Chelsea, whose parents died at ripe old ages, the death is not devastating—but the mourners still need to process their grief. Not everyone reacts to death in the same uniform way. When in *silent* mode—alone— the mourner has the time and space to reflect on genuine feelings, rather than being assaulted by a consoler's view of what they *might* or *should* be feeling.

While in the traditional sense I didn't have this opportunity to lament silently, the most natural progression for me, upon hearing of the death of my father, was isolation and silence for 48 hours. I did not want to engage with anyone other than my family. So I withdrew into myself. This element of grieving brought harmony to my inner and outer reality.

As previously noted, my father died in New York on a Saturday. We had to make arrangements to fly him to Israel for the burial. We buried him on Monday, but if the burial had been in New York, it would have been Sunday and with that, the shiva would have commenced. With the delayed burial, the "silence" precedes. None of my family members were afforded the opportunity of silence in the first three days of after my father's death, since we were traveling to

Israel from all four corners of the world. Our "silence" time was mostly while traveling to Israel.

I boarded the plane from Heathrow Airport in London. I had a middle seat between two young men. I closed my eyes. I shut down. Silence. I didn't try to be silent, it just was. I just allowed it to move at its own velocity. Unaided and undisturbed, the silence unraveled the agonies of the conflicted feelings of grief. It was instinctive to me, although I learned later that Jewish mourning regards this as prescriptive.

Death is the division of two: separation of body and soul, and a separation between two people. That type of separation naturally leads you to feel isolated, both symbolically as well as physically. Just a few days earlier I had been with my father, now I was not. I had a whole routine around him—visiting him and talking with him— and now I did not.

The silence and isolation are an important stop on the path of mourning; however, it is only a step along the way. At day three of the *shiva,* it's prescriptive for consolers to come and get you out of the silence. Too much silence for too long can result in the world becoming tighter and closer, until you feel paralyzed.

Prior to the burial, my father was the focus for compassion. As soon as *shiva* started, we, the mourners, were the focus. My father was the victim of death, and we were the survivors of it. Now the role reversal—we were visited and tended to. The comforters become the comforted. The Torah refers to a mourner as an *avel (ah-vel)*, which means withdrawing. Clearly this infers that a mourner has a desperate need for silence for a short time, and then it instructs the comforters to relieve the solitude, and draw them out of their confinement.

This silent turn-around gently navigated me, us, through the turbulence to where we could stand again on firm ground. The ground where my father was buried. The ground that was slowly compacting down on my father's body. Emerging from the silence, I became ready and welcomed into the next phase of *shiva*—storytelling—even my own story of the experience that I had just lived through. It was time to be comforted.

Healing through Storytelling

To resume a quality life, mourners are told by Jewish tradition to be a "receiver of comfort"—that is to receive and not resist the comforting words of visitors, the suggestions of well-meaning people who come bearing compassion. My friends' and relatives' visits were like medicine, and I accepted the gesture more than the words of consolation. They gave me the opportunity to reminisce and to express feelings. In fact, neuroscientist Paul Zak has found that hearing a story (in my case, hearing my own story)—a narrative with a beginning, middle and end—causes our brain to release cortisol and oxytocin.[2] These chemicals

2   Paul J. Zak. . The Moral Molecule: The Source of Love and Prosperity (New York: Dutton, 2012), 76-77,

trigger uniquely human abilities to connect, empathize and make meaning.

It was a never-ending tragic carnival, in a way, where with each person I changed up the story a bit. But with each audience, I remembered in more detail—and learned from it. Our stories can be lessons in objectivity. Also, sitting with my siblings and sharing stories, each one of us added more detail. This brought my past from black and white to color. It united us, as we took turns sharing our versions of the past and understanding it. The process was purging and extremely exhausting, but it was meant to be that way. It was to break down the barriers, the ego, and let the mourning flow.

Reflecting back on the narration of my father's life, his care for the community ultimately contributed to healing my past with him. If it were not for the visitors coming together for my dad's *shiva*, I may not have heard these positive remnants of my father's past. Some of these memories were stored in the caves of my mind, and seeing people that I have literally not seen since elementary school brought them back. My nursery school teacher (from 40 years ago!) came to visit. The comfort of having Rise there was like having a warm cup of milk. Since my parents traveled so often when I was a young girl, and my mother knew that I had a special relationship with her, she asked her to take care of me during the summer when I was five years old. Rise, who was single at the time, took me to her parents' country home in upstate New York. I was ill during that time. It was quite usual for me to come down with the flu every time my mother went away, and that was often. It felt like abandonment, although Rise did take tender loving care of me.

Business associates of my father and old family friends came to the *shiva* and shared stories of how my father helped them get their start in business, or how he helped my relatives purchase their first home. When I heard these stories, I was able to re-frame my past, my pain, and recognize that my father was on his own journey in this world, as we all have our own personal voyage. It helped me forgive.

He left an indelible imprint on all those he helped. That my childhood was "sacrificed" in a sense, made my embittered past with him more palpable. It was for the greater good. There was meaning in his death. Now I was to make meaning in my life.

I can empathize with mourners who feel isolated if no one is visiting—feeling that no one understands them or wants to be around them. Incidentally, this is where *The Mourner's Prayer* (see section on *The Mourner's Prayer*) can be very helpful. Usually, the loneliness is the worst part of the grief. The *shiva* is designed for visitors to lift you out of your distress and talk with you about the deceased, during a time when most people would not even ask or inquire. Now is the time to share with others. In sharing our story, we dissipate our pain, little by little, giving a small drop to each person.

Death has a way of being linked with repentance.

The sitting and storytelling might make us think about our regrets in our relationship with the deceased. We repent for not appreciating all that our loved one had to offer. Sometimes we even repent our lack of ethical living or religious ritual. Often after the death of a loved one, a mourner may do a 180-degree character turnaround. I know many people who became more religiously inclined, even more so when there was absolutely no religiosity within the family. Sometimes, it's a way to continue life by connecting to our ancient religious past.

Throughout the *shiva* when we were all sharing stories about my father, it put into sharp focus the fullness of his life and what he left behind. This became a philosophical, existential endeavor. What is it that I will leave behind for the next generation? What will be my legacy? Who would come to my *shiva*? What would they say about me? How will I make my life meaningful, and have bearing in this world? Life is fleeting, and death puts you face to face with man's search for meaning.

The Sabbath

All *shivas* pass through the Sabbath—the culmination of the week. It is such a holy day that we are commanded not to sit *shiva* during the Sabbath; however, it does count as a day within the week of mourning.[3] Judaism in its implicit reverence for life instructs the bereaved to sanctify the

---

3   Moed Kattan, 14b-16a. Mourning is suspended for Shabbat and for certain holidays. The obligation of rejoicing with the community takes precedence over the obligation to mourn.

Sabbath, and death to sit in the back seat for 25 hours.

For the Sabbath, we were allowed to remove our torn clothing and change into clean clothes. We were encouraged to leave the house and go to prayer services in the local synagogue. I was happy to sit at home and do nothing, so exhausted was I. Later on, after the Sabbath meal, we all took a long walk together and it felt recuperative, just being out in the fresh air on a silent Sabbath evening.

Leaving the house for the Sabbath services can be a healthy step back into life. At Friday evening services in some synagogues, mourners enter the sanctuary only after the singing of *Lecha Dodi*, a hymn welcoming the Sabbath. I was part of this awesome experience once, when I accompanied my sister to Friday night services after her husband passed away. We stood behind the closed doors of the Sanctuary, and after the *Lecha Dodi*, the doors were opened, and all the congregants stood up. The rabbi announced my sister's loss, and we walked into the Sanctuary. The empathy in the room was palpable. I will never forget that experience of awe and tenderness.

You don't need to belong to a synagogue to attend services. A synagogue belongs to every Jew. After services, members of the congregation approached my sister (whether they knew her or not) to offer condolences.

The last few years of my father's life, my brother and sister and I made every effort to come to my parent's home for the Sabbath. It was the one day that my father forced himself with every ounce of will in his frail body to get up and sit through the meal—that's how important it was for him. That we came to be with him gave him all the more power to sit at the table with us. Thereby, the seven days and the passing of Sabbath without my dad sitting at the head of the table made the death more of a reality. The fact that my dad did not return for the Sabbath solidified his absence; that he was never coming back and his seat at the head of the table would forever be empty.

The Mourner's Prayer

The Mourner's Prayer is often referred to as Kaddish, an Aramaic prose poem that is recited by mourners, traditionally within a presence of ten voices, three times a day for eleven months. Interestingly, Kaddish makes no reference to death or mourning. Rather, it is a poem reminding us that God is beyond us, understanding is beyond us, holiness and beauty are all around us, but we have work to do. There is hope, we are still here as a link in a chain to continue in spite of the despair to bring Godliness—peace to this world, peace within ourselves and peace within our families. Life goes on.

Every day during the week of shiva my brothers, Gideon and Jackie, stood facing east (toward Jerusalem), wearing colorful Bukharian threaded yarmulkes, leading the prayers in the front of my aunt's living room. Behind them were about 20 men, praying with them and bolstering them through the hard process when all my brothers wanted to do was just retreat into themselves. There was something so raw about the way it was recited, the way my brothers were singled out to lead it. And somehow everyone was familiar with this prayer, like a haunting Jewish anthem. It was an experience of the senses, where like music it penetrated and vibrated in the most primal way. The rhythmic interplay between my brothers and the congregants responding "amen" felt hypnotic—the encounter transcended words. With every "amen" it felt as if they were lifting us. It was palpable. The "amen" affirmed that "we are here for you and our collective energy will lift you." My brothers ended by taking three steps back—back from the spiritual world to the physical world.

I knew the prayer from synagogue services, but now every time I hear it, it's a mantra of sadness and a personal petition for peace and completion. This prayer makes me well up.

Kaddish Transliteration

*Yitgadal v'yitkadash sh'mei raba b'alma di-v'ra
chirutei, v'yamlich malchutei b'chayeichon
uvyomeichon uvchayei d'chol beit yisrael, ba'agala
uvizman kariv, v'im'ru: "amen."
Y'hei sh'mei raba m'varach l'alam ul'almei almaya.
Yitbarach v'yishtabach, v'yitpa'ar v'yitromam
v'yitnaseh, v'yithadar v'yit'aleh v'yit'halal sh'mei
d'kud'sha, b'rich hu,
l'eila min-kol-birchata v'shirata, tushb'chata
v'nechemata da'amiran b'alma, v'im'ru: "amen."*

Y'hei shlama raba min-sh'maya v'chayim aleinu
v'al-kol-yisrael, v'im'ru: "amen."
Oseh shalom bimromav, hu ya'aseh shalom aleinu
v'al kol-yisrael, v'imru: "amen."

Translation

*Glorified and sanctified be God's great name throughout
the world which He has created according to His will.
May He establish His kingdom in your lifetime and during
your days, and within the life of the entire House of Israel,
speedily and soon; and say, Amen.
May His great name be blessed forever and to all eternity.
Blessed and praised, glorified and exalted, extolled and
honored, adored and lauded be the name of the Holy One,
blessed be He, beyond all the blessings and hymns, praises
and consolations that are ever spoken in the world; and say,
Amen.
May there be abundant peace from heaven, and life,
for us and for all Israel; and say, Amen.
He who creates peace in His celestial heights,
may He create peace for us and for all Israel;
and say, Amen.*

The Fellowship of the Mourner's Prayer

Kaddish is a prayer where the mourner is suddenly forced to the front and center of the community to lead the congregation. You might wonder why. Someone who has just lost a family member may want to withdraw and become invisible. Perhaps even the tragedy of the loss makes them lose faith in God. Sitting in the background and just mumbling words, is not being actively involved. Rather, as the mourner, you are the leader. Just as you might question your faith in God, the answer is to lead and pray. Everyone is relying on you. You count. In response, the community responds, "amen." That "amen" is an affirmation that you are not left alone to fend for yourself, but the community is here to cushion you. Furthermore, since the mourner is the one who has experienced the death, it is also the mourner who understands the meaning of human existence more than anyone else at this moment. Touching death touches the fragility of life.

Additionally, that "amen" is a declaration between parent and child that Judaism lives from generation to generation, from rituals to merit. By reciting a prayer that elicits a communal response, it elevates others to the majesty of God. This majesty creates a society in which the parent and child exist and experience reciprocity at a macrocosmic level.

In the first week of mourning, Jewish ritual says that the community comes to you—we are here to comfort you and give you that boost to lead the prayers. This is also done to ensure that for the week of shiva, the mourners do not have to leave the home where they are best able to fully experience the mourning process. They do not have to dress up to go out, or put on a public face for anyone.

It is certainly appropriate and poignant to have services in the home itself, for the center of Jewish life is the home. This is the place where Jewish values are passed down. This is where family celebrations take place and where joys are shared. It is also where pain and loss are shared. It is where Judaism lives even in death.

This is a gradual process of reengaging in life. In some communities, there is the custom where at the second week, the mourner goes to synagogue but does not sit in his or her usual seat. Life is not the same, and the displacement of the seat exemplifies that. The third week, he goes to synagogue but this time sits in his seat yet talks to no one. There is a gradual process of reengaging with the community. The fourth week, after the 30 days, you may sit in your seat and talk to people. From isolation to a point where the community lures you back into the world— the work of mourning is about returning to life. It is the praxis of moving from isolation back to a vital part of the community.

Furthermore, when everyone in the congregation sees you are leading Kaddish, they know you are a mourner— you are singled out. The beauty is this unity creates a wellspring of support. When a mourner is absent from the Kaddish, the community seeks them out. Numerous accounts record the camaraderie that mourners previously unattached to the Jewish community form during the days of grieving. The congregants offer strength and support just by sheer numbers. Mourners who start coming to services to say Kaddish sometimes become involved members of the community to remain connected. It's one more example of how mourning customs promote a healthy way of processing the death of a loved one within the embrace of the community. My brother Jackie has become more observant as a result of saying Kaddish every day in synagogue, while developing a fellowship with the congregants. The poignancy of it all is that the mourner can show up somewhere every day in the midst of the chaos of grief and be given hope that order will return. It also creates the space within each day to remember the deceased and then return to life.

Getting Up from Intense Mourning

It was the seventh and final day of intense mourning. It was time to move to the less intense mourning period. I was still wearing that gray jersey dress that had been torn at the burial. I was glad to get out of that dress already. It was at the height of summer, and after a week it did not smell like a bouquet of flowers. Maybe more like wilted flowers.

After the morning prayers, we sat only for a few hours (although it counted as a whole day) and then got up from the low stools. The first thing I did was change into clean clothes and throw away the dress.

I did not know at the time that there are many rabbinic authorities that deal with mending the garment, rather than throwing it out. For the loss of a parent, the garment may be mended back together, albeit with crooked stitching, since life is never the same again. In hindsight, I wish that I had kept the dress. I did not have the insight then. It would have been a good memorialization—a demarcation in time and place of this shiva experience. I imagine that I would have worn this dress at my father's yahrtzeit every year.

Wearing my clean clothes, I walked, starting from the right side, around the block of my aunt's home, where we had sat for seven days. A beautiful tradition in Judaism is that the walk around the block symbolizes the mourner's return—our return—to society following the intense mourning period. The concrete act of physically stepping outside, changing scenery, walking around the block, and coming back in, says that this house and our relationship with this house will now be renewed. The circle around the block is an allusion to the concentric circles of mourning, where at each stage, the circle widens to more latitude. Funny enough, the block itself was not a block. The apartment where we had sat was located on a circular roundabout. We literally walked around in a circle. Just like the egg we ate, and just like the circle of life. We start where we end.

When I returned back to New York after the shiva and turned on my local cell phone in the airplane, it was ringing and beeping with text messages of condolences. At my front door, the mail brought news from friends and members of my synagogue. Members, people who I did not even know, sent me condolence cards and tributes to my father's soul. I was humbled, mostly because so much of the mail was from people I had never even said hello to. I did not even know they knew I existed! I received a call from the past rebbetzin (wife of the rabbi) of the synagogue, who was 90 years old. She made it her priority to call all mourners, even ones she did not know. Sadly, a few months later, she died too. As a side note, this is why it's so crucial to be part of a Jewish community, so that you are never left in isolation. I learned long ago that Judaism is not meant to be practiced alone; you have to part of a community responsible for one another and cohesive in times of good and bad.

After the Week

Jewish mourning is a process of stages. It's not an on/off switch, but a gradual process of grieving, accepting and finding meaning. There is a residue of mourning after the week to always remind you that this time is different than all other times. It's also a notification to your friends and community when you are not around, bringing awareness that a death has taken place. We all need to be sensitive to each other's pain and loss. After *shiva*, the intensity of mourning is reduced for the next 23 days. However, some restrictions continue to remain in effect:

- New or ironed clothing should be avoided. If needed, one may have the clothing worn by someone else for a few moments so it's not "new" anymore. This does not apply to undergarments.
- Bathing time should be reduced.
- Haircutting, shaving, or cutting one's nails should be avoided if possible.
- Avoid activities that are not in the spirit of mourning, such as listening to music, pleasure trips, social events, buying and redecorating a home.
- One may go into a marriage ceremony before the meal is served and while no music is being played.
- If one's profession is such that he must attend festive events for his income, he may attend them.

STAGE THREE

◄•————————►

The Thirty Days

The first 30 days following the burial (which include the shiva) are called shloshim, from the word meaning "thirty." Why 30 days? The Jewish calendar is marked by lunar time. As the moon waxes and wanes in a cycle, the 30-day period of mourning is an opportunity to emotionally come full circle. The process begins with the funeral and first days of shiva, when not even a glimmer of light is seen. As time goes on, there is a transition at each Sabbath where the light slowly comes back, fuller and fuller. The 30 days is an important central cycle of time, a time to renew and to come to grips with a new reality.

Most restrictions that applied to mourners during the seven-day shiva period are now lifted. For the next 23 days, mourners are allowed to leave their house and begin to work again. One is still mourning, but during this period the laws allow for a gradual reentry into everyday life.

FOR 30 DAYS, I did not cut my hair and my brothers did not shave. Moments of deep sadness and longing were to be expected, and having these few restrictions reminded us, and the people around us, that this process was certainly not over. It was not a period of self-deprivation; rather, there was tenderness to this reality. The Jewish sages knew that to get up from the shiva and jump back into a normal routine would not be healthy. We were still mourning, even though the intense pain had now become more bearable. The unshaven face is a physical sign that the mourning is still in process and real. Although it was not apparent by my physical looks that I was in mourning, it was apparent that my brothers, Gideon and Jackie, were by their unshaven faces. Anyone who did not know that my father had passed and saw my brothers immediately knew to ask if they had lost someone in the family. The growth of the beard is the call for people's sympathy—tenderness is shared between mourner and consoler.

Of course we still felt the pain of the loss but Judaism recognizes that, to a certain degree, the passage of time eases and heals the pain. Being able to return to everyday life freely helps achieve this healing. The shiva was the worst period, the 30 Days was very hard, but with time, it gets easier

The 30th Day

Traditionally, families gather on the eve of the 30th Day to share support, recite prayers and Psalms, and to give charity in memory of the deceased. Why charity? I can relate to that concept. My father was a charitable person. I remember as a child sitting in his office on school vacations where various Jewish organizations would come into the waiting room of the office asking for money. My father said something to me that I will never forget. "If someone can bring themself to ask for money, then you must give, even if it's ten dollars. Always give something. Make them feel good." Since my father was no longer alive, these charities lost a donor. To memorialize my father and elevate his soul, my siblings and I had a responsibility to continue to give.

We rented a hall in the synagogue and invited 200 people for a sit-down meal. It was an evening dedicated to memorializing my father's life. A basket was passed around from table to table to collect for charity. We had noted rabbis from the local community. There was a microphone for anyone to share a story about my father. Aside from the rabbis, who spoke about how my dad started the first Afghan synagogue in Forest Hills, my son Jonah gave a speech. He shared with us his feelings for my father and ended with a tear-jerking remark: "My grandfather was the father to the fatherless." Jonah learned just prior to making the speech that my father had looked after and guided through life two of my first cousins, who were orphaned at a young age. Jonah related to them, as my ex-husband was an absentee father to him. He felt my father had been the only man who looked after him, even after I married my second husband. This was comforting to me, since I felt my father was very absent for most of my life, and yet he had provided that anchor for my son.

Spouse Comes out of Mourning

Upon 30 days after my father's passing, my mother came out of mourning. For the spouse and siblings, mourning is 30 days. The idea behind a widow mourning for 30 days is that they don't have to do nearly as many rituals to memorialize their spouse, because they lived with them. The widow feels the absence more profoundly than anyone else, because they shared a life, a bed, stories, secrets, laughter and sadness.

Spouse Searching for Purpose

As I write this, way past the year of my father's passing, my mother, 81 years young, is fraught to find her purpose in life again. Her main objective in living was to care for my father, and prior to that his parents, her own parents, her six sisters and brother, and her synagogue, all under the umbrella of matriarch of the family. With my father's death, my mother felt as if she had lost her job in this world. She became a bit more frail, embittered, anxiety ridden and a hypochondriac. I affirmed to my mother several times that I understand it's not easy losing a spouse; however, if you are still alive, that's God's way of saying, "You matter and there is still work left for you to do here." This is the time to share your wisdom and give it to your community. Before my father passed, he was concerned about leaving my mother. In fact, I believe that part of the reason he outlived the doctor's prognosis for his "death date" is because he was afraid my mother would fall apart. My mother needed to hear that my father would not want her to stop her life after his death. She agreed.

Although she is struggling with finding her new identity, she has taken some strides to ameliorate the anxiety. For one, she is selling her McMansion home and downsizing to an upscale apartment building in Miami where she has an instant community of like-minded people. She takes classes of interest and has found some friends to take long walks on the beach. I suggested many activities to my mother: volunteer work, joining a recreational club, taking classes at the local Jewish Community Center. My mother understands that she has to rely on her community to propel her and find purpose again. For the time being, she is managing and moving forward.

My mother rummaged through the closets of yesterday. She examined my father's things, which held the stories of my father's past. She took an inventory of his life, as each piece held a story. He was a collector of the latest gadgets; items you would find in the Sharper Image, although he bought them long before they ever reached that store. He bought them during his 50 years of traveling. On Saturday nights, my father would wear an ascot with an art deco black onyx and diamond pin. There was a large collection of his ascots, ties and alligator belts, hundreds of new socks that I helped my mother organize. We sorted it all into piles and decided which ones to disperse to the grandchildren. My mother donated many of my father's belongings to Jewish charities. She passed down some special mementos to the grandchildren, so she can see them wearing my father's personality—a remaining connection from one generation to the next. That was one of her ways of honoring her husband. On the one hand she is letting go, and on the other she transfers some of the residue to her grandchildren so they will have a piece of my father. It is an ongoing process and I am proud of her.

STAGE FOUR

◄──────────────►

The One-Year Period

During the 12-month period from the day of death, only one who has lost a parent is still considered a mourner. Why this extra stage of mourning only for a parent? Typically, our parents die when we are adults and out of the house, living on our own or with our own families. Mourning a parent who may not have been an active part of our adult lives may require more of the ritualistic mourning procedures to consciously remind us of their absence. Psychologically and spiritually, our connection to our parents is the essential relationship that defines who we are as people. Therefore, the loss of a parent requires a longer period of adjustment.

I PLAYED PIANO as a child, and sang blues and jazz well into my adult years. Music was always playing in my home and car. For one year, every single time I got into my car, I thought about my dad through the void of not having the radio on. In the case of no music for the year, it was a time of reflection and facing my thoughts about my father nearly every time I got into my car. He was with me the entire year post death.

Although I was not regarded by my father as "daddy's little princess," and he was not the type of father who sat me down and gave me advice or guided me through life, with his death and the year that ensued I was on a feverish, unconscious search to fill the void. One of the ways I did this was by participating in and creating events that were geared toward people similar to my spiritual epicenter—hungry for knowledge, growth and transcendence. In a sense, I was looking for a home. The void and the search were calling me back home, the longed-for home I wish I'd had when I was a child.

The Year to Reflect

The first year is a year of *uninvited* firsts. The first Sabbath without my father, then the first holiday with out my father. The first time I didn't attend family celebrations with live music. The first time I didn't listen to music. The first time I avoided shopping for clothes. I did not do everything in its totality to the letter of the law. I did the best I could, and at each first I thought of my father.

After the loss, things are not the same. They are not as they were, and that needed to be dealt with, regardless of the fact that my father died at a ripe old age. I realized that the solace that mourning provided would be lost if I attempted to resume normal life before properly mourning. It is for this reason that our Jewish sages advise not to make any major changes in one's life. They understood that mourners might be inclined to keep busy in order to avoid the grief; therefore, it is generally unwise to change homes, mates and even friends during this period of readjustment. To delay grief with busy work is to live with it sitting in the background, simmering until it boils over.

Certainly, mourners will find comfort in keeping busy, but self-generated change only adds stress to a system already overloaded with psychological and emotional instability. I saw this firsthand with my mother, who was so anxious after my father died that she was pushing herself to sell her home before she was psychologically ready. She was also looking to move to Miami. All reasonable and understandable acts, but it was too much too soon, and she was having anxiety attacks regularly. Accelerating change increases vulnerability and makes the world seem like it is moving at an uncontrollable pace, where there is nothing safe. Furthermore, there is no way to focus on mourning when you are running from pain; you will only get smacked by it in the long run.

In reality, if you don't mourn, grief will inevitably seep into you in a primal, unruly and unhealthy way, regardless of whether you had a good relationship with your deceased parent or not. Death of a family member cuts into you in ways that you don't even realize, and it's usually worse if there were unresolved issues, as in my case. I found it helpful to reflect on the positives, and what I would like to carry on from my father. The residue he left behind generated a deep state of gratitude for all he tried to give me, in spite of his limitations.

As children, we spend most of our lives in "taking mode," and our parents, being parents, are almost constantly in "giving mode," whether we recognize it or not. It is hard to say thank you from a taking perspective. In a relationship where parents are taken for granted, this period of time helped me to focus on recognizing the good he desperately tried to give in the best way that he could with the tools he had. I emphasize "with the tools he had," as I believe everyone is trying to do their best with what they have.

Parents also represent values and ideals. They are God's representatives to us in this world. They impart essential tools for living. This extended period of mourning recognizes that the loss of such a relationship has deep spiritual ramifications, no matter what the relationship was like.

Without the full year of mourning, with all its stages, it is difficult for me to imagine how someone can move through the complexity of feelings surrounding death. The full process gave me a way to feel some peace while maintaining a continuous partnership with my dad, as well as a renewed harmony with God—a God that permits loss and even created it into the blueprint of existence.

STAGE FIVE

←————————————————→

Death Anniversary

The death anniversary can be a time where family and friends gather to speak about the past year without the deceased, and remember all the years with the deceased. As the year-long process of mourning comes to a close, there is a letting go. Although it might have the same mechanics as the initial week of mourning, where family and friends came to pay respects, the extreme sadness is not as pronounced. There is some healing, and at this point in time the mourner is more inspired to take on some traits or endeavors to keep the memory of the deceased alive. While the person is physically dead, the mourner—who has come out of mourning, out of a fog—can now internalize the deceased in a way that carries on through them. The mourner can now absorb the messages of life and death, take the lessons of their loved ones to heart and ensure the memory of the departed is honored properly.

IT IS SIGNIFICANT to note that in Judaism we downplay birthdays, never commemorating the date of birth of one who has passed away, yet we are careful to mark the anniversary of someone's death. King Solomon, author of Ecclesiastes, relates a parable comparing this practice to a ship.[1] How odd that we hold a big party when the ship is about to sail, yet when it arrives at its destination, nothing is done. It really should be the other way around.

Although the day of birth holds all the potential for the life that will be, the day of death is the marker of who we actually became. Our worth is measured according to how much of our potential was realized. Did we live up to who we were, to the best of our ability, in the time that we had?

When our loved one dies and goes back to God, to their "port of call," we mourn that we no longer have them here with us. Yet we remember what they were able to accomplish in life. The death anniversary, known in its Yiddish term as *yahrtzeit*, is a time to feel the sadness, but also to memorialize who they were and the life they lived.

The death anniversary is a yearly spiral continuum

---

1   Midrash Kohelet on Ecclesiastes VII.

where we revere the memory. It is designed to stoke the memory with an annual revisiting of the loss. The yahrtzeit is a touchstone—to remember, honor and find solace, in order to transition from the past to the future. To look to the future means to truly live a meaningful life. It is also an enduring glory of the parental heritage, a day set aside to contemplate the quality and lifestyle of the deceased, and to dwell earnestly upon the lessons they have transmitted.

Unveiling

Since ancient times, it has been the custom to mark the grave with a stone or monument.[2] The marker or monument serves to identify and give an address to the grave so that relatives will find it when they visit, honor the memory of the deceased, and identify the place for burial. The service of commemoration or unveiling is a formal dedication of the monument. It is customary to hold the unveiling within the first year after death.

The psychological benefit of having a "mark" to visit is for solace and comfort. Underneath the stone is our loved one, and there is quasi-feeling of "home" to that—home is where our family is. It is a place where we want to be silent and contemplate. Being there reminds us of what our loved ones stood for, the values they cherished and the legacy they left us. Sometimes just being in the presence of their

---

2   After Rachel died, "Jacob erected a monument on Rachel's grave" (Genesis 35:20).

grave brings mystical revelations to our encumbered lives.

At the unveiling of my father, we brought a bucket of water and washed the tombstone, as a sign of respect. The tombstone should never be dirty; it symbolized how we are all tenderly looking after him, still.

Within the Jewish faith, it is customary to leave a small stone on the grave. We placed a small stone upon the gravestone as a sign that we were there. We, who are physical, need a physical act to express the reality that we were indeed there. The simple stone, a symbol of eternity, represents our eternal devotion to upholding the memory of our beloved. Stones are fitting symbols of the lasting presence of the deceased's life and memory, rather than flowers that wilt.

There are many symbolic reasons as to why we place a stone on the grave. I like the explanation that the rabbi officiating the unveiling at my father's tombstone offered:

"In Hebrew the word for stone is 'eh-vhen,' spelled aleph-bet-nun. These letters symbolize the person's perpetuity—aleph is for Av, the father; bet is for ben the son; and nun is for nin, the grandchild. This is what the deceased leaves behind, a continuation of family and Judaism—the pulse of life. Of course, there are those who die and leave no child or grandchild, but there is something very poignant here if we look further. A person can leave behind good deeds, no matter what age, and this has lasting effect—just like a stone, an eh-vhen."

Washing Hands at the Cemetery

Before departing the cemetery, we wash our hands at a water station. Each one of us first pours a cup of water, once on the right hand, then once on the left, alternating three times. Jewish ritual dictates that whenever we touch "death" we must wash our hands. We don't dry our hands, but leave them wet and turn the cup upside down after washing, so that the memory of the departed lingers on the fingertips.

Gathering

It is customary on the *yahrtzeit* to have a gathering with friends and family in honor of the beloved. My family and I traveled to Israel for the unveiling. After the cemetery, we commemorated my father with a luncheon with my first cousins in a winery overlooking the Judean Hills. All sides of this huge dining hall were encased in glass so the sun beamed through. The long dining table seated all 40 of us rather comfortably. I sensed my dad shining his presence on us. I knew how truly fulfilled my dad felt (and my uncle Mayer, who is with him) that my cousins (whom he was extremely close to) and I were all together for a meal in his honor. What a beautiful Jewish tradition, that we got to do something that comforted us, and equally pleased my father. We reflected on the essence of his mission in life and what he accomplished. Reminiscing about my father reaffirmed how our connection to him would be never lost

STAGE FIVE Death Anniversary

as we proposed toasts in his honor. We had not spent this quality time together with my father's side of the family in at least 25 years. From the other world, my father and his brother united us all.

Customs on the Day of the Death Anniversary

We commemorate our loved ones each year on the Jewish anniversary of death. Here are some of the customs on that day:

- Light a 24-hour yahrtzeit candle at home the night before, because the Jewish day begins in the evening. The candle is lit in accordance with the biblical verse, "the soul of man is the lamp of God" (Proverbs 20:27). In other words, the candle is a reminder of the body's departure, but the soul—the light—still shines. That's why it's customary to recite the blessing upon lighting the candle: May his/her memory be a blessing.

- Give to charity in your loved one's memory. The lesson of sharing and giving to those less fortunate is a way to connect the deceased to you and to the charity. When my father died, I donated to Birthright, an organization that offers a free trip to Israel for all Jewish young adults who have never been there.

- Study Torah that day. Read from a book about Judaism or Torah ideas, or arrange to learn with someone from the community. Since my father's death, I have become a Partner in Torah (Jewish learning over-the-phone or in person with your personal Torah trainer) with a student who lives in Los Angeles. We communicate weekly over the phone and we discuss the weekly Torah portion and its relevance to contemporary times.

- Recite The Mourner's Prayer. If you cannot, arrange for someone to recite it on your behalf.

- Sponsor a kiddush in synagogue on that day, or on the preceding Sabbath. I have found that sponsoring a kiddush is a way to unify my community. This has special meaning to me since my father, while living in Bangkok, provided meals to travelers every Friday night at the local synagogue. It brought people from all walks of life together with a shared intention for the Sabbath.

ANNUAL
COMMUNAL
REMEMBERANCES

By remembering, we process our loss and achieve a modicum of tranquility. Healing comes as a result of confronting and resolving loss, not from escaping and avoiding it. We stop on these major Jewish holidays four times a year to remember—to cherish the memories, affirming the presence of our loved ones. This communal remembrance summons us to remember their lives; it is a connection to generations past and loved ones gone.

THE ANNUAL COMMUNAL REMEMBRANCE is known in Hebrew as yizkor, "to remember." With the memory of a parent, you transcend the physical world in which you dwell into the spiritual one to which they have ascended. As you connect to them through your memory of them here in this world, so do they connect to you.

Yizkor is based on the firm belief that physical acts of goodness can elevate the soul of the dead. There is a profound beauty in Jewish tradition: Even though your parent is gone from this world, there is always something you can do to elevate their soul through the celestial planes. It is concretized through prayer, and charity that we give in their memory. Any bit makes a difference, as long as you are giving and reaching.

Charity is not measured simply by material resources, but also a generosity of spirit and temperament. When we prompt our memory of our beloved, we think not only about who they were, but also about who we are. Not only about what could have been, but also about what still can be. Not only about what I should have done, but also about what I still have the ability to do. In this way, we make the Yizkor prayers we recite, and the memories we cherish, serve as not only a link to the past but also a bridge to the future. And in so doing, with generosity of spirit, we bring new meaning to old memories, and merit to the souls we remember through our own inner expansion.

Yizkor also stimulates acceptance and continuity at each juncture of its recitation. With objective time, we remember selectively, which can be therapeutic in times of grief. When we consciously remember or are least prompted to remember, we spark "episodic memory," rather than a mere fleeting memory.[1] Episodic memory is the salient memory of an event in a period of time, place and emotions. It allows an individual to figuratively travel back in time. Instinctively, we seek to remember the good old days, even if they weren't all that good. The positive outcome of this "episodic memory" is that we learn to retain memories and re-envision the intimate experience with our beloved. It's our way of cherishing in order to move on, knowing that we can always tap into the plethora of our memories.

This can also be an opening to allow new loves in our life. Knowing that we can retain the memory allows us to concurrently move forward. That is yizkor: to remember and never forget, to contemplate and to move on to the next juncture.

When is Yizkor Recited?

Yizkor is recited after the morning Torah reading on Yom Kippur, on the last days of Passover and Shavuot, and

---

1 The term "episodic memory" was coined by Endel Tulving in 1972. He was referring to the distinction between knowing and remembering. Knowing is more factual (semantic) whereas remembering is a feeling that is located in the past (episodic).

on the eighth day of Succot, called Shemini Atzeret. It is recited on these days even if they fall on the Sabbath, a time when memorials are otherwise inappropriate for the festive nature of the holiday. In most synagogues it is recited after the rabbi's sermon.

You might wander why yizkor is a communal event specifically centered around the major Jewish holidays. The answer is embedded within the question. Holidays are a time that can be particularly dreadful for those who have lost a loved one—a modern psychological term for this is the "holiday blues." Our wonderful Jewish sages knew that holiday times bring back only too well memories of joyful times spent with departed loved ones. Thus, they built specific days of mourning into the holiday cycle, providing outlets for renewed grief during the Jewish year, within a community context for support.

Also, during Temple times, Jews would make the pilgrimage to Jerusalem on these major holidays with fruits of their first yield. It was required to bring the best and in abundance to donate to the Cohanim (priests) working in the Holy Temple. This is yet another reason why it's appropriate to give charity in memory of our beloved. The commemoration is a link to the past and the charity we give is a link to the future.

◄———————►

I remember my first yizkor distinctly. It was on Yom Kippur. I was sitting in my synagogue and all congregants who were not mourners were asked to leave the sanctuary. More than half the people in the synagogue left. Suddenly, an eerie silence filled the room. A vibrant space, just moments ago pulsating with social zest, was transformed. A sense of mystery, awe and dormant pain surfaced. You could cut the rawness of the emotions with a knife. Something profoundly authentic united all those standing in the room.

My heart shifted to my late father. I remembered.... He opened a synagogue at his business office in Bangkok, Thailand, and made the seemingly impossible possible. He believed that if an idea or a person came to him, then there was a reason it did and he acted upon it. It illuminated for me how we can all appear as random people moving around in this world, but we all matter. Every single one of us is a piece of the mosaic, with our own unique ways of elevating this world.

Memorial Candle

It is an ancient custom, on the four holidays when yizkor is recited, to kindle a memorial (yahrtzeit) candle for the departed before the onset of the holiday, that will remain lit through the yahrtzeit. If possible, it is best that the lights be flaming wicks, as opposed to an electronic yahrtzeit lamp, since the flame and candle symbolize the relation of body and soul.

GRIEF AND
GOING FORWARD

Everything has an appointed season,

    and there is a time for every matter under the heaven.

A time to give birth and a time to die;

    a time to plant and a time to uproot that which is planted.

A time to kill and a time to heal;

    a time to break and a time to build.

A time to weep and a time to laugh;

    a time of wailing and a time of dancing.

A time to cast stones and a time to gather stones;

    a time to embraece and a time to refrain from embracing.

A time to seek and a time to lose;

    a time to keep and a time to cast away.

A time to rend and a time to sew;

    a time to be silent and a time to speak.

A time to love and a time to hate;

    a time for war and a time for peace.

–Ecclesiastes: Chapter 3

CENTURIES AFTER King Solomon wrote Ecclesiastes, the famous folk band The Byrds commercialized this psalm with a song called, "Turn! Turn! Turn! (To Everything There Is a Season)," which reached #1 on the Billboard Hot 100 chart of music in 1965. What exactly did The Byrds (or rather King Solomon) tap into that resonated so strongly with the public? It's a song that everyone can relate to. Everything has its time and place, as it's part of the natural order of the world. We need to make room for life, with all its passages, and death to turn, turn, turn.

The Jewish sages instituted a one-year process of mourning—a structure to let mourners feel their aloneness, separating them from the outside world, and then gradually reinstating them back into society. When the year is over and the mourner comes out of the prescribed time of mourning, it's time to dance again, to laugh again, to plant again—to move on. In fact, Jewish law mandates that a mourner may not mourn past the year, so as not to strain the mourner's mind to retain the active memory of the death. We could not survive if we were always stuck in the past. If such memories hung around in our awareness all the time, it would paralyze us; however, if we didn't deal with it altogether, it would paralyze us just the same. God did not create humans to suffer, but to mourn at the appropriate time and then live in light again.

That does not mean that moving on means forgetting about the deceased. There will always be a space inside for them. Time does heal, but not because we are busy and the memories fade. With time comes objectivity. We realize that the person we are now is the result of the loved one we lost. The elements of our character, actions and values all result from this special soul and the experience of loss.

I believe after death there is still the possibility of continuing their lives, their words that need to be said, through us. By embodying the conversations, and the thoughts that manifest as actions, their soul is re-energizing you. This is what's meant by the saying, "The beginning of thought is the end of deed."[1] In other words, when your mind puts into action a positive deed, you eternalize the deceased.

Ultimately, we have to work toward a place of transcendence, a place where we have risen above the loss, a place where we gain a new perspective. Transcending loss is about striving to make the experience an ultimately positive and redemptive one. It is about using our pain and challenges in a meaningful and inspirational way. It means making the best of a sorrowful situation and letting grief be a teacher.

---

1   Ma'arekhet ha-Elhout (Mantua, 1558), f. 36a.

My father's death has created a void, a healthy void that has catapulted me to be more serious about my spiritual growth so that I can channel that feeling of loss in a tangible, meaningful way. For me, it was a time to mull over my father's characteristics and good deeds. I asked myself what I could integrate of him into my being. During the year of mourning, I finished up my second book, Spiritual Kneading through the Jewish Months: Building the Sacred through Challah. I dedicated the book to my father, a homage to his legacy and to his many Jewish causes.

George Pollock (former director of the Institute for Psychoanalysis in Chicago), a psychiatrist who did a psychological study on personal transformation, coined the term, "Mourning-Liberation Process." He analyzed artists, scientists and other professionals who had been impaired by grief. What he discovered is that creative personalities all demonstrated that creativity can clearly be a direct outgrowth of bereavement. He concluded that successful bereavement might well result in increased creativity. This may very well explain my creative personality. I have suffered many painful losses in my life and my coping/ grieving process has always been to create. I can't say this is a conscious effort. It just is for me. I believe it is a way for me to fight back the void and recreate an acceptable version of my life situation. Transforming grief liberates.

It has also invigorated me by lifting me out, and challenging me to push forward. To find the depths in me that I have found in the darkness. The blackness of death has created a fissure. The light finds its way through the rupture; the way water stealthily leaks its way into a hairline crack. I seek out from where the light emanates. Oddly enough, the light of transcendence is within me. It has been within me all along. Teaching Torah, leading challah bakes,[2] and visiting the homebound elderly are just some of the ways that the year of mourning has engraved and etched a part of my father onto my psyche that will forever carry through me.

Grief does not end with burial. It does not ever end at the 30 days. It doesn't end ever, I think; it just shifts. And if mourning is done honestly, healthy sublimations from the void can surface—actions or thoughts that embody the deceased within you in a positive way. Through my father's death I have learned that time is fleeting, so we must try to live with courage, kindness, laughter, honesty and humility.

I will end with a traditional farewell said to mourners. It conveys positive feeling with layers of deep meaning. This farewell is a formula that relies on God to console, whereas comfort is humanistic. As mourners we may have a hard time receiving personal words from our peers, but an invocation from God as participatory in the mourning is transcendental. This phrase moves the mourners away from the self and connects them to all those who have

---

2 I teach challah classes pulling from Jewish texts to enhance a women's spiritual growth via the tradition of challah baking while meditating upon the Jewish theme of the month. Refer to my book, Spiritual Kneading through the Jewish Months: Building the Sacred through Challah (Shamashi Press) 2014.

experienced mourning. It exemplifies the universal need for mourners to share their grief with the interconnectivity of all mourners. We are not alone. You are not alone. May the Almighty comfort all the mourners of Zion and Jerusalem.

GLOSSARY

Amen–a declaration of affirmation.

Aramaic–ancient Semitic language closely related to Hebrew.

Avel–what a mourner is referred to after the burial.

BCE–before common era of the Gregorian calendar.

Brit milah–Bris. The covenant of circumcision.

Challah–traditional bread for the Sabbath and Jewish holidays.

Chevra kadisha–Jewish Holy Burial Society

Cohen–the Priestly caste

Conservative–a religious movement developed in the United States during the 20th century as a more traditional response to Reform Judaism.

Halachah–traditional Jewish law contained in the Talmud and its commentaries.

Onein–a mourner during the period immediately following the death and prior to the funeral.

Orthodox–Jews who follow traditional Jewish law.

Kaddish–the Mourners Prayer

Kiddush–has multiple meanings. It is the blessing over wine said on the Sabbath and on Jewish holidays. Additionally, in many synagogues, morning services are followed by a reception. Since it is preceded by the blessing over wine, the reception is often called a *kiddush* as well.

K'riah–the ritual tearing of garments prior to a funeral.

Midrash–rabbinic interpretation where the rabbis filled in the gaps found in the Torah.

Mikvah–ritual bath.

Minyan–a prayer quorum of ten adult Jews.

Mitzvah–a sacred obligation designed to connect the person to the act and God.

Niftar–death, as in released from duty in the physical plane.

Parsha–the weekly Torah portion. They are 54 parshas throughout the Torah.

Passover–a holiday celebrating a commemoration the Jewish liberation by God from slavery in Egypt and their freedom as a nation under the leadership of Moses.

Psalms-the first book of the *Ketuvim* ("Writings"), the third section of the Hebrew Bible. The book is an anthology of 150 individual psalms, authored by King David.

Rabbi-teacher. In modern times a rabbi is a seminary-ordained member of the clergy. In ancient times, the rabbis refer to the wise men who codified the Talmud.

Rebbitzen-wife of the rabbi or female religious teacher.

Reconstructionist-a religious movement that began in the United States in the 20th century by Mordechai Kaplan, who saw Judaism as an evolving religious entity.

Reform-a movement that began in 19th century Germany that sought to reconcile Jewish tradition with modernism. It was an entry point for German Jews to assimilate into German culture.

Seudat havra'ah-meal of consolation served to mourners upon returning from the funeral home to the shiva house.

Shabbat-Sabbath. A day of religious observance and abstinence from work, kept from Friday evening sunset to Saturday after sunset.

Shabbat Chattan-Aufruf (Yiddish), which means "calling up," is the Jewish custom of a groom being called up in the synagogue for an *aliyah*, i.e., recitation of a blessing over the Torah.

Shavuot–the word *Shavuot* means weeks, and the festival of *Shavuot* marks the completion of the seven-week counting period between Passover and *Shavuot* when historically it is the time the Jews received the Torah at Mount Sinai.

Shemini Atzeret–the day after *Succot*. It's a holiday extending *Succot* for a more intimate celebrated day, because God enjoys our company so much that He requests we stay another day in holiday mode.

Shiva–the seven-day period of mourning following the funeral.

Shloshim–the 30-day period following burial, which includes the seven days of shiva.

Shomer–a Jewish legal guardian entrusted with the custody and care of an object or person. A *Shomer* is entrusted to watch the dead body until it is buried.

Shul–synagogue.

Shulchan Aruch–Code of Jewish Law written by a 16th century rabbi named Joseph Karo.

Siddur–prayer book.

Succot–*Succos*. It is the festival known as the Feast of Booths, giving thanks for the fall harvest.

Tahara–before the body is buried, it is washed in a ritual act of purification.

Tallit–prayer shawl.

Talmud–oral laws of the Hebrew Bible that was transmitted through oration and later written in 200 BCE to 500 BCE.

Torah–the first five books of the Hebrew Bible, divided into 54 portions that are read aloud and studied in an annual cycle.

Tzeddkah–charity.

World to Come–usually refers to one of three things: the way the world will be in the End of Days when the righteous are resurrected; a world of immortal souls that will follow the age of resurrection; or a heavenly world enjoyed by righteous souls immediately after death (i.e. prior to the End of Days).

Yahrtzeit–the anniversary of death.

Yarmulkes–skull cap.

Yizkor–communal memorial prayer.

Yom Kippur–Day of Atonement. It is the holiest day in the Jewish year.

RESOURCES

Jewish Burial Society

The National Association of *Chevra Kadisha* (NASCK) is a united group of Jewish Burial Societies in the United States and Canada, dedicated to traditional Jewish burial practices. It acts as an umbrella organization to assist Jews in the entire burial process, from pickup to burial to *shiva* assistance. http://www.nasck.org/find.htm

Jewish Funeral Directors of America

Database of national Jewish funeral homes in the United States. https://www.iccfa.com/groups/jfda/memberdirectory

Locating a Service for Kaddish

- The MyKaddish.com website offers a phone tutor to learn everything you need to know about *kaddish*. This same website also matches you up to a synagogue, according to your Jewish comfort level, specifically for reciting *kaddish*. www.mykaddish.com
- Worldwide prayer database, where with a click of a mouse, you can locate a prayer service close to anywhere you are. Many of the services are not just in a synagogue but a workplace, office or restaurant. More often than not, the services are for the observant Jew,

but you will find that many people are there reciting *Kaddish* just like you. Orthodox Prayer service close to anywhere you are: www.godaven.com/kaddish.asp

Find a Synagogue

Locate a synagogue according to the tradition of Judaism you observe:

- **Union for Reform Judaism (URJ)** is a network of nearly 900 Reform congregations across North America. Their progressive, inclusive approach unites thousands of years of Jewish tradition and values with modern Jewish experience. http://www.urj.org/
- **The United Synagogue for Conservative Judaism (USCJ)** is the main organization leading the practice of Conservative Judaism in North America. The database contains over 675 congregations. http://www.uscj.org/
- **Orthodox Union (OU)** is the Union of Orthodox Jewish Congregations of America, embracing over 400+ Orthodox synagogues from all across North America. https://www.ou.org/
- **Chabad** offers a directory of the Chabad Lubavitch centers around the world. These centers offer Torah classes, synagogue services and assistance with Jewish education and practice. http://www.chabad.org/

Yahrtzeit Calculator

The death anniversary of a loved one's passing is a time to remember the person, in the synagogue, by reciting the *kaddish* prayer, through the giving of extra charity and through learning. Determine the date of your loved one's passing for this year.

http://www.chabad.org/calendar/yahrtzeit_cdo/ aid/6229/jewish/Yahrtzeit-Calculator.htm

Books

The Jewish Way in Death and Mourning by Maurice Lamm

This book provides readers with comprehensive information about traditional Jewish mourning rituals and customs. Lamm primarily covers Ashkenazi mourning customs commonly practiced in the United States.

A Time to Mourn, A Time to Comfort by Ron Wolfson

When someone dies, there are so many questions, from what to do in the moment of grief, to dealing with the practical details of the funeral, to spiritual concerns about the meaning of life and death. This indispensable guide to Jewish mourning and comfort provides traditional and modern insights into every aspect of loss. In a new, easy-to-use format, this classic resource is full of wise advice to help you cope with death and comfort others when they are bereaved.

Bereavement Group

A bereavement group provides a kind of fellowship and support founded on shared experience and understanding. Groups help mourners explore the wide range of normal grieving and share strategies for learning how to reintegrate into the world.

A wonderful website with many resources, including locating a grief support group: http://thegrieftoolbox.com/

Acknowledgements

My inspiration for writing this book came to me by my special friend, S.S. It was easier to see the speck in your eye, which was just a mirror to my own unfinished mourning. I wrote this book for you and everyone like you who did not know why and how to mourn.

I want to thank all the people that have read this manuscript several times and provided illuminating feedback:

Marjorie Maltin, with your insightful heart, told me how I was missing in this book at its initial stages. You inspired me to go back, revisit psychological issues, and share myself for the service of this book.

Arthur Kurzweil, for reading my manuscript line-by-line providing crucial feedback that seriously shape shifted this book. From spiritual insights, to my target audience and book layout– you gently veered me to share my unfiltered soul. There is no way this book would have read this way without you.

Margot Atlas, good friend and board member at the Shalom funeral home in Chicago. Your input was another mosaic to this book. Thank you for introducing me to Mindy Botbol, the funeral director at Shalom Funeral Home.

Mindy, if I did not know you were a funeral director, I would have mistaken you for a psychologist. The Shalom funeral home is lucky to have such a tender and caring heart oversee the sanctity of the dead body and bereaved families.

Rabbi Kara Tav, Chaplain at Queens Elmhurst Hospital, amidst supervising your chaplains and crazy hours at work, you took extensive time to go through every line for accuracy. Was I lucky!

Jerry Weinstein, head of the Chevra Kaddisha in Great Neck, who took several hours from his day to sit with me and go through the manuscript, line by line for technical issues.

Lewis Aron, director of the NYU Postdoctoral Program in Psychology for your beautiful and thoughtful blurb and for directing me to two professional articles on the psychology of Jewish mourning by Joyce Slochower: Out of the Analytic Shadow; On the Dynamics of Commemorative Ritual and Mourning & Holding Function of Shiva.

Thanks to my respected friends and colleagues who gave me their time to review this manuscript for feedback and completeness. Jennifer Artley, Charlotte Kashani Etti Samuel, Dana Lustbader MD, and Chaplain Daniel Coleman.

My editor, Dawn Raffel who said such impactful words to me about this book that just encouraged me to produce the best concise work I could, "I wish I had this very book when I lost my parents."

Joanna Brown, my book layout designer for the second time around. Between juggling your kids, husband and life we made a beautiful book.

Alisa Roberts for your keen eye in picking up the minutest spelling errors. You polished my book.

INDEX

About the Author

Dahlia Abraham Klein is a published cookbook author, Silk Road Vegetarian: Vegan, Vegetarian and Gluten Free Recipes for the Mindful Cook (Tuttle, 2014) and Spiritual Kneading through the Jewish Months (Shamashi Press, 2015). She has been conducting  Spiritual Kneading classes privately and at synagogues of all denominations, teens and adults in her Long Island, NY community since 2010.